Memories of Mount Hawke

Clive Benney & Tony Mansell

First Published November 2008 by Trelease Publications

Copyright © Clive Benney & Tony Mansell 2008
All rights reserved

15 Kerensa Gardens
Goonown
St Agnes
Cornwall
TR5 0YX

Design by Daniel Benney
www.danielbenney.co.uk

ISBN 978-0-9545583-7-6

Printed by R. Booth Ltd
Printers & Bookbinders
The Praze
Penryn
Cornwall
TR10 8AA

Contents

Introduction

Mount Hawke is the second largest community in St Agnes parish, it lies
to the south of St Agnes village, a couple of Cornish miles from the sea at
Porthtowan. Wikipedia, the online encyclopedia, suggests that together with
those two villages, it is known as the *Golden Triangle*. Why that name we are
not sure but its roots are firmly embedded in mining; it was for that reason
that it was created.

Access to the village is by one of three main routes but there are others...
narrow roads that wend their way through the old wooded valleys of Banns,
Manor Parsley and Menagissey. The main ones carry much more traffic than
a few years ago, a reflection of how the village has grown.

    Of these, there is the road from St Agnes, which passes the old Railway
Station, takes a right turn at the bottom of the hill and eventually leads to
a valley known as Gover. The old Congregational chapel once stood in the
field to the right and some way over the hill to the left is the new Skatepark.
On the far side of the valley is a turning to the right, this leads, via a narrow
road, up past the old and the new schools and into the village.

    From the Truro direction the long narrow road from Two Burrows
crosses a bridge which once spanned the railway, where trains departed
Mount Hawke Railway Halt for the main line. About half a mile further,
in the triangle of land on the right, is a retail outlet, where George and
Stephens once sold their cars. To the left is the Church of St John the Baptist.

    The road from the sea at Porthtowan travels through a derelict mining
valley, past Navvy Pit and up into the village via Short Cross, at the west end.

Despite its industrial history there should be no expectation of finding any
working miners in Mount Hawke, those that toiled in the local mines disappeared a long time ago. They have left us their rows of cottages, their chapel
and the now silent remains of their mines... at Tywarnhayle, Ellen, Music
and elsewhere.

There are many who mourn the passing of the old Mount Hawke, the tight-
knit community where they knew everyone by name and where much of the
work was on their doorstep. The entertainment was home-produced and the
church or the chapel was central to their way of life. But nothing is forever
and, while it is good to reflect on the past, we have to look forward. Mount
Hawke is a lively village with a beating heart.

Local history is best written by someone *on the ground,* with a first-hand knowledge of the area. Quite apart from it being one link in a chain of books covering the entire parish, both authors have connections with the village. Clive Benney was born at the other end of the parish but married into a local family and for a number of years was responsible for policing the village. Tony Mansell spent most of his young life in Silverwell but lived in Mount Hawke for eight years in the 1970s and his mother still lives there.

We have collaborated on a number of projects and this is the fourth book written in partnership. We continue to produce books under our own names while working together to collect and record the history of the district. We share a passion for our area and of anything Cornish so the motivation to research is ever present. Add to this our enthusiasm for the written word and an unrivalled collection of parish photographs and you have a unique formula for providing a record for future generations.

We hope you enjoy reading about this fascinating area of Cornwall, the places, the buildings, the businesses and perhaps most important of all, the people.

The Village

With its narrow streets and old cottages you would be forgiven for thinking that Mount Hawke has a long and ancient history. It certainly has pockets of antiquity but the village itself is comparatively young, it developed in response to the demands of the mines…in the 1700s.

It must once have been a familiar sight to see miners trudging the roads, making their way to a gruelling day's work at one of the mines dotted around the area but now the machinery of that once vibrant industry is silent. Ironically, despite the demise of mining, the village has continued to grow.

The main street too is different as the gentle pace of the horse drawn vehicles has given way to the motorcar, that blessing and curse of the 20th century. As in most villages vehicles now line the streets and dominate the scene, a fact lamented in the Women's Institute scrapbook of 1950.

The village is large enough to support its shops, not as many as a few years ago but still there and trading despite the pressure from the supermarkets. It has its pub, and its chapel & church still call the faithful to worship.

No part of St Agnes Parish has grown more rapidly than Mount Hawke. Just why it was chosen for this huge expansion we are not sure but during the early 1970s it was transformed from a sleepy Cornish village into a large community with sprawling estates on its periphery. There was a particular concern that one of the developments was to have its own community centre, a fact that seemed designed to divide the old village from the new.

Whether or not those fears have been borne out, it is a fact that even before 1970 the village had changed. Many farms had disappeared, some of the old shops had closed and small housing developments had spread out across what was once agricultural land. Areas just a short walk from the main street had been transformed and would have been unrecognisable to the old miners.

It is indisputable that Mount Hawke is now a very different place but it is far from being a retirement village; it is a vibrant community with a good mix of ages. The physical alterations are there to see, to be applauded or criticised, but perhaps the biggest change is in the people; the culture is different, the Cornish accent is now a rarity and the dialect is fast disappearing. But that applies throughout the parish, indeed throughout Cornwall, in that respect Mount Hawke is no different to any other community.

Circa 1905…The leisurely pace of life in Mount Hawke

Historian Ashley Rowe commented that Mount Hawke differs from most Cornish villages in that it has no early history of association with church or manor. *"It is a mining village of comparatively late origin like numerous other villages in the county but, unlike them, it has survived the decay of the mines… Goon Prince, a name found on 18th century maps, was almost all unenclosed land, stretching from the modern Mount Hawke to Three Burrows. About 1753 the demand for copper caused Truro adventurers to seek out possible mining grounds and the hillsides of Banns, together with sites on Goon Prince, was much in demand. About this time Prince Royal copper mine was opened, the workers of which built cottages on copyhold sites obtained from the Tywarnhayle Manor"* Mount Hawke, though not yet called by that name, came into being.

Local place names are always of interest and we are grateful for the opinions of Peter (Nick) Thomas and Oliver Padel. As ever, the place names are a mixture of Cornish and English.

The Mount in Mount Hawke is thought to indicate its elevated location, relative to the land on most sides. The prefix Mount is quite common in Cornwall and Oliver Padel thinks that its use in front of another name might have been an attempt to make it look more French and, therefore, more up-market.

Many sources claim that the Hawke came from an important family who lived there from the 1750s. The church logbook of 1902 supports this by stating that it was derived from a family of rope manufacturers called Hawke and that Mrs Walters, widow of the late R Walters, was a descendant of that family.

Banns is a much older area and nestles in a valley, to the north of the village; it is mentioned in many ancient documents. An extract from the 1650 survey of the Manor of Tywarnhaile, or Tiwarnhaile, refers to *"Free tenants of the said Mannor… Henry Edmonds gent holdeth to him and his heires for and from seven years to seven years according to the custom of the Manor by the surrender of James Kent one third part and the moiety of another third part of one messuage and 24 acres of land English in Bans except a Mill called a Stamping Mill…"*

Banns is thought to have derived from the Cornish word *pans* which means hollow, dingle or dell. It would have been an bans or, in English, The Dell. An, or the, was dropped to give us Banns.

Circa 1900…The valley at Banns

Gover Valley is on the road from St Agnes. It is a little further upstream from Banns and Trenithick Mill; their hills are more or less parallel. Gover is simply the Cornish word for stream; to use these old local names is to use the Cornish language.

Croft Prince: The Cornish word *croft* means *uncultivated enclosed land, rough ground,* and the Cornish word *Pryns* means *Prince.* It is written in a Cornish word order, viz. Croft Prince rather than Prince's Croft and translated it means something like Prince's rough field. As to the identity of the prince, we have no idea. It could possibly be a name rather than a title but we have not found any examples of that surname in Cornwall. There are other locations with prince in the name e.g. Goon Prince and Princes Common and the likelihood is that it relates to the princely ownership of the manor of Tywarnhayle which had possession of the area in question.

Manor Parsley is to the far west, on the Wheal Rose to Porthtowan road. The words are English but the order of use is Cornish viz. Manor Parsley rather than Parsley Manor. We do not know why it was so named; perhaps it was the surname of someone who lived there or maybe a plant which grew in profusion in the damp location. The plant likes rich soil that does not dry out so the area in this valley may well have suited it. Parsley is apparently notoriously difficult to germinate and an old saying suggests that germination is slow because the seeds had to travel to hell and back two, three, seven, or nine times (depending on sources) before they could grow. (That's about as much horticultural information you're likely to find in this book).

   Kelly's directory of 1906 lists someone living in a house called *Manor Parsley* and Thomas Tonkin, in 1712, lists one of his tin-bounds as *Roman's House* alias the *Mannor of Pasly.* Parsley does appear on earlier maps but its claim to be a Manor is extremely dubious, as you will read later.

Menagissey is located on the road from Manor Parsley to the west end of Mount Hawke and, like so many places in Cornwall, it is difficult to determine when you have passed from one to the other. It is an attractive name, often confused with Mevagissey in books and directories.

   It certainly has the feel of being a Cornish name but there is little doubt that it is a corruption as from the late 13th century to the early 17th century the area was known as Milgysy or Milgisy. The Cornish word for kennels, specifically for hunting-dogs, is indicated as the origin of this name and it may well have been the location of a kennel for the Duchy manor.

Park Shady is that lovely valley between the village and Towan Cross. The spelling on the direction post is *Park* but it often appears as *Parc*. The reason for the name will quickly become apparent. It is a walk amongst the shadow of the trees; to be enjoyed by all ages and many a young couple have been teased about going courting down Park Shady.

Maurice Bizley refers to some of these areas in his book *Friendly Retreat:* Bans, Banns or Bands from 1386, Gover from 1516, Croft Prince from 1842 and Menagissey in all its guises … Melgisey, Milgisie wartha, Menagesey, Molgysy, Melgysy, Milgisy, Melgisey, Menegissey or Menagissey Moore … from 1315.

In 1845 the population of Mount Hawke was 3,000, a considerable village. The Women's Institute scrapbook poses the question of where they all lived but then answers its own question by explaining that there were many more people per house and numerous cottages have now disappeared. In Gover Hill valley, near the present waterworks, there are traces of a number of cottages and whole rows have been demolished including where The Village Stores now stands.

The book also refers to possible traces of Bronze Age habitation in the fields to the west of Church Hill and of Iron Age sites further down the stream. It states, *"There was probably a Celtic village here, as on the high ground, east of Mount Hawke Halt, there are burial mounds."*

Businesses & Services

Businesses spring up from time to time, some flourish, some do not. Occasionally they remain and pass down through the generations while others continue their existence with new proprietors.

We have made no attempt to include them all but we do hope that the next few chapters convey the range that existed in Mount Hawke; of course, some are still there.

As in most communities, many goods and services were once available on the proverbial doorstep, certainly to a much greater extent than today. People lived, worked and played within their own village.

Before the days of easy transport, and the birth of the supermarket, local shops served the needs of the village folk, many operating out of the front room of an ordinary house. These were family businesses, often run by wives and daughters.

Information from trade directories provide us with many names and dates and to this we can add information from other sources including the memories of some long-standing members of the community.

We start with a simple list; it is somewhat unsatisfactory as no locations are given. We then move on to cover others in more detail. No doubt there are some that will surface after we go to print…they always do.

James Garland, linendraper and grocer…1856 and 1862.
William Henry Garland, druggist…1856.
Francis Gill, grocer and linen draper…1856 and 1862.
John Goyne, grocer and linen draper…1856 and 1862.
Joseph Gribben, shopkeeper…1856, 1862 and 1873.
Thomas James, butcher…1856 and 1862.
John Libby, grocer and linen draper…1856, 1862 and 1873.
John Nettle, tailor…1856, 1862 and 1873.
William Richards, grocer and linen draper…1856 and 1862.
William Henry Bennett, draper and grocer…1873.
Mrs Sarah Garland, grocer and draper…1873 to 1902.
Mrs Phillipa Goyne, grocer and draper…1873, 1878 and 1883 (also post office from 1878).

Charles Garland... 1878 and 1897 (also post office for part of this time).
George Chellew Moyle, butcher... 1878.
James Nicholls, shopkeeper and coal dealer... 1878.
John Phillips... 1878 and 1883.
Henry Richards, grocer and draper... 1878.
William Sampson... 1878.
Henry Walters, grocer and draper, Menagissey... 1878 to 1889.
Mrs Betsey Williams, grocer and draper... 1878 and 1883.
Mrs Eliza Gribben, pork butcher... 1883.
Mrs Elizabeth Nicholls... 1883.
Mrs Sarah Richards... 1883 to 1889.
Mark Richards, pork butcher... 1889.
Mrs Eliza Richards, pork butcher... 1893 to 1902.
James Dunstan... 1914.
Mrs Elizabeth (Bessie) Jolly... 1914.
John C Pearce, butcher, Higher Banns... 1919 to 1923.
Sargeant Randall, grocer... 1923.
Miss Phyllis Tonkin, grocer... 1923.

The Bottom Shop: Mrs E (Bessie) J Grigg ran the grocery shop just above the Women's Institute hall. She was there for many years, certainly from the 1880s to 1922. The property is now a dwelling but the style of the front window testifies to its former use.

We are not sure if Bessie was the first proprietor or whether she took over a going-concern but when she retired due to ill health her relative, Edith George (née Williams b. 1886), continued to run it. It was listed in trade directories from 1923 to 1939 as *Wesley George, grocer and provision dealer.* A notice on the stable door stated that the bottom section should be kept closed, to keep out the dogs. Dried cod was stored in bundles against the wall and Edith kept a large knife with which to slice off an onion or a piece of cheese. Wesley was also a farmer, at *Wingfield,* the land at the rear of the shop. From here he produced the milk for sale across the counter and on their round.

Edith and Wesley were the parents of Mary and Donald George; Mary still lives in the village. Edith's father had been one of the early proprietors of the horse-bus service, during the 1870s and 1880s.

Circa 1900...The bottom shop with probably Bessie Grigg in the dark dress

Mary George (b. 1920) recalled counting the coupons during the Second World War, when so many things were rationed. She said, *"I can still recall the names of some of our suppliers: Amos Jennings and Nortons from Truro, Trounsons and Willy Bishop from Redruth and Vivian of Camborne, for bed linen. Bread came from Jack Cowling, the village baker, and a large loaf sold for 4½d."* Brother Donald recalled that the pasties were pretty good too. He said, *"I always had one on Mondays as I didn't enjoy Sunday dinner leftovers."*

The family moved further up the village in 1946, to live in the bungalow *Carn View*, from where they continued farming.

Donald George (1924 to 2008) recalled one hairy experience at *Wingfield* when he was sailing his model boat in the water tank and over-reached himself. He was convinced that their next-door neighbour and *second mother*, Mrs Blackney, saved him from a watery grave. When the family ceased farming Donald became an agricultural contractor and worked for many of the local farmers; he also set up and ran the local garage.

Mr and Mrs Gooding then took over the shop and with their daughter Marion ran it for the next 11 years, until the Hutton family came on the scene.

Mavis and Clive Hutton moved from Birmingham in September 1957. Mavis recalled that they moved in at three o'clock and took over with no instruction whatsoever. She said, *"Mr Gooding simply said that he would call back after a few days to see how we were doing. Mrs Dell was our first customer, she came in for something or other but I think that what she really wanted was to check us over. Our second customer was Mrs Cowling. She announced that she hadn't come to buy anything, she simply wanted to know if we were church or chapel. I said, 'Oh, the same as you.'*

We began sorting the shelves and moving stuff around but when we shifted a bag of potatoes the next customer fell through the floor; it was covering some rotten boarding.

We had a few disasters including when the Weights and Measures chap condemned our scales. And there was one lady who used our shop to hide from the bailiffs. Stanley Tonkin often came in to buy one Aspro; we used to keep an open pack on the shelf just to supply him.

Trounsons of Redruth supplied most of the things we sold but I bought some items from the large shops in Truro. Littlewoods sold very good bacon and I regularly bought 7 lbs to re-sell in our shop. One particular lady came in just to buy bacon. Her comment was that it was much better than the stuff where she worked… at Littlewoods. We became a SPAR shop, the first in Cornwall.

In 1958 Clive bought a mobile shop but while he was delivering in Mawla the handbrake slipped and the vehicle careered into a bullpen, that was the end of that. We left the shop in 1962 and Clive then worked for Mother's Pride for a few years."

Mavis & Clive Hutton in their shop doorway chatting to a visitor
…a couple of other families have run it since then but for many years now it has been a dwelling

Mount Hawke Stores: A little further up the hill, almost to the road junction with Penhall Lane, there was another grocery shop…at *Trefalghun House.* Mrs Muriel Rowe and her daughter ran it for many years; they were Ashley Rowe's mother and sister. Mr Bamford was the last person to trade there as a grocer, that was in the 1950s and early 1960s. At times he widened his range of goods to include anything which he thought might sell including new bicycles.

When his van was stolen in Redruth the Police were called in to trace it but were unaware that he had recovered it himself…until they arrested him for stealing it. Bamford's Bridge is a location not too familiar to many, except maybe the regulars of the Victory Inn back in the 1960s. Alfie Johns said that the little bridge at the bottom of Banns always presented Mr Bamford and his van with a problem but strangely it was always on the way home.

Mount Hawke Stores in the 1950s

The (LONDIS) Shop: John Martin Uren was a shopkeeper in 1906 selling items of drapery and groceries. By 1910, and up until about 1923, Mrs Emma Uren ran the business. We assume that she was his wife and that he was involved in some other activity or that he had died.

The postman poses with the children for the photographer outside Mr Uren's shop sometime around 1906

Mr and Mrs Richard Arnold James then took over and for many years the shop was one of the main providers in the village. They carried out some alterations and during that time the chalet at the rear was brought into use as a temporary shop. Their advertisement included the line *Motor for hire*.

Gladys Thomas' earliest memories of the little shop are in the 1930s when there was a tin box in front of the counter. Under the glass lid was a pile of pink wafer biscuits and she said, *"I always wanted one."*

This photograph is from the time when Mr James ran the shop

A later view of the shop with its modified front

Ted Murray and his daughter, Eileen, bought it in 1952 and stayed for the next 25 years; towards the end of this period it became a MACE branded.

D (Don) & T A Stevens then took over and during their long stay they enlarged the shop.

Circa 1980...The shop in Don Stephens' time

During the 1980s the Miller and then the Jackson families were behind the counter followed by Mr and Mrs Price who were the proprietors for about ten years during the 1990s. Mr & Mrs Russ McKenzie then took over for a couple of years followed by the current proprietor, Martyn Norris; he has been there since 2003.

The Village Stores is a busy shop but with a shorter history than many of the others. Before it was built the site was already the location of commercial activity including a mangle house, tailor's shop and possibly a school, these are all mentioned elsewhere. They were in a row of buildings set at right angles to the road and facing where *Greenacres* now stands.

Edwin (Neddie) Mewton married a butcher's daughter…Jessamine (Jessie) Harris from St Agnes and joined the family business. They decided that Mount Hawke had some potential after taking some surplus meat there to sell. Sales must have been good because they decided to build a lock-up shop, next to the old blacksmith's. This was sometime around 1930 and within a few years, and certainly by 1935, they built a bungalow there.

Neddie Mewton's lock-up shop

Their eldest daughter Lorna was born in 1931, at St Agnes, and in 1939 they had their second daughter, Edwyna; she still lives in Mount Hawke.

Lorna recalled helping her father on the meat round on Saturdays when they delivered to Barkla Shop and Mithian. She said, *"In the early days he slaughtered his own animals but later on he bought the meat from wholesalers."* Gerald Tonkin helped Jessie in the shop in the early days while Neddie was out on the round; he later combined this with running a threshing business.

In 1961 Neddie was taken ill and was no longer able to continue; Monty Burrows, who had been working for him since he left school in 1958, took over the round. When Neddie died in 1963 his wife continued with the business and Edwyna, who was by then married to David Hall, lived there and helped in the house leaving Jessie free to run the shop and Monty, the round.

Within two or three years Monty took over the business, his parents moved in to the bungalow with him and Jessie moved to *The Nook* but continued to help in the shop. David & Edwyna moved to *The Elms* and, in 1987, to a bungalow in Henly Drive.

Monty said, *"I worked for Neddie even before I left school, in the business and cleaning his beloved steam engine. I hated the oil and dirt and I think cleaning the brass put me off anything to do with steam for life. Shar and I were married in 1970, we increased the size of the shop by extending into what was the bungalow front room."* In 1978 they sold the business to Shar's cousin, Martin Caddy who, with his wife Gill, ran the business until about 1984. Mr & Mrs White then took over but their involvement was brief and Bob and Jan Hanson bought it in 1986. They were there until 2000 when it was taken over by Chris and Anthea Cox, the current proprietors.

The butcher's shop with the attached bungalow

Circa 1980...The shop at the time when Martin & Gill Caddy were the proprietors

Trelawney Cottage: In 1923 Mrs Uren and her daughter, Mabel, moved from the shop in the square and opened another, at *Trelawney Cottage*. It sounds as though this was a short-lived venture and when Mabel took a job in Redruth her mother ceased trading and sold the property. The only other public use for the premises seems to have been as a venue for whist drives.

Edith and Alfie Johns lived there many years later and remember the parquet floor in the shop area with the bare concrete around the perimeter, where the shelves were positioned.

Tallack's Shop: Later in this section there is an item about an ironmongery shop in Rope Walk, nearby was another grocer's shop. In an interview with Shirley Barrett, Nellie Pearce recalled that it was run by Olga Grant's grandmother. The Brooke-Bond Company and Trounson's steam wagon made regular deliveries of produce up the narrow lane. Shirley also spoke to Olga Grant who told her that her uncle, George Tallack, was involved with the shops. She said that the flour was delivered in big linen bags, currants in wooden boxes and tea in wooden chest with silver lining. Her granny ran the shop and also killed pigs and sold the pork out of a bucket which she carried around the village.

Circa 1900...Tallack's wagon loaded with corn outside *Old Oak* cottage

The Post Office: In the early days the post was sorted at Scorrier and brought to the area by the post cart, a red box on wheels drawn by a pony; Mr Hodge drove it. Once transferred it became the responsibility of the village postman whose round was lengthy and included many muddy lanes. Solomon Tregay was one of the earliest postmen. He was a man who took his official capacity seriously and if asked to deliver a message to a neighbour would refuse to do so unless it was written and stamped. As a carrier of Her Majesty's Mail he considered that he should not convey any unofficial communications. The friendly chat over a cup of tea was also shunned and he would not enter a house for any purpose whatsoever. (W I 1950)

Postman Solomon Tregay

Bill Morrison was the sub-postmaster at St Agnes from 1962 to 1983 and was well placed to record the story of the postal service in the parish. In the 5th Journal of the St Agnes Museum Trust he wrote, *"To meet the increased demand, post offices opened in smaller villages: Mount Hawke by 1883; Porthtowan 1893; Blackwater 1897; Mithian 1906. In 1889 Peterville had a wall box and by 1895 there were boxes at Mithian, Towan Cross, Gover, Trevellas, Goonbell, Goonvrea and Vicarage Road."*

Bill's article has also been raided for information about the early sub-postmasters and mistresses; this has been augmented by trade directory entries and personal memories.

In 1878, and at least until 1883, Mrs Philippa Goyne was the *Receiver of Mail* (officially a post office in 1883); she also ran a grocer's and draper's shop. The Ordnance Survey map of 1880 appears to locate this a few doors down the hill from the present post office but this may be bad cartography and the Goynes may have operated from the building at the entrance to Rope Walk, where the post office was a few years later. Mrs Goyne received the post from Scorrier Sorting Office at 8.30am and dispatched it at 3.15pm; if money orders or the services of the telegraph office were required then customers had to make the trip to Scorrier.

Chas Garland was the *Receiver* in 1889 and probably up to 1906. Postal Orders were issued there but not cashed. By 1897 the despatch of the post was at 4.10pm and 6.45pm ... the service was improving.

Circa 1900 ... The post office and shop in The Yard

Mrs Mary Chynoweth (née Menadue) began her long role as sub-postmistress in 1906. By then the location had changed, the office was in middle cottage of the row in the LONDIS shop square, set at right angles to the road. The post arrived from Scorrier Sorting Office at 7.35am (including Sundays) and 2.10pm and was despatched at 7.45am and 2.15pm … Sundays 12 noon. Blackwater was now the nearest point for money orders but Scorrier was still the telegraph office.

The post office in the square … just up from the chapel

Mary and her husband, Henry, had returned to the village in the 1880s, from the USA where he had been a miner. In 1891 he had left again, for South Africa, but this time he went alone and did not return; he was killed in Johannesburg in 1899.

In 1940 Bert Kalber moved from Towan Cross and re-established the post office in The Yard, where it is now. After just a year it was taken over by Mrs Nellie Pearce, a real village character. Nellie was from Menagissey and her husband, Harold, was from the far side of Banns; he ran the local taxi service. She was very involved in village activities through the Women's Institute and the Gardening Society; her name appears throughout this book. Bertie Thomas delivered the post around this time; he was deaf and dumb.

The post office back in The Yard in the 1940s

When they retired, in 1965, Nellie and Harold moved to *Ilfra* (a house at the top end of Rope Walk, named after the resort of Ilfracombe) and their daughter-in-law took over.

Christine moved to the village in 1952 when she married Claude Pearce. She had worked at Chacewater Post Office for a couple of years and at Mount Hawke as holiday cover. At first she continued to sell stationery and drapery items but sometime around 1970 she restricted the business to the post office service. The private library also ceased, a service which Nellie had provided.

Christine recalled that February 1971 was a testing time; it was then that the switch to decimal currency was made. *"To prepare us for D Day we had three nights of training but it was not so much a case of understanding it ourselves, it was more to do with helping the old folk; it was very confusing for them."*

Sorting and delivering the post was a large part of the job and the *posties* at that time included Bill Herman, Maurice Williams and Mrs Hilda Harding (later Clements). Joe Penhaul also helped with the delivery at sometime.

The Yard in the 1960s with the post office on the left

Maurice Williams was in trouble on one occasion … for emptying the post box at Navvy Pit. He hadn't bothered to put on his uniform and the Police were alerted to a suspicious character tampering with Her Majesty's Mail. In the mid 1970s local involvement in the mail ceased, it was undertaken direct from Truro.

The telegram service received maybe two or three messages a day. They arrived over the telephone and were written out and despatched by whoever was available, in the school holidays that meant Neil Battersby from Towan Cross.

The post office premises were leased from Francis Garland and it is likely that his family had owned then since 1889 or before … when Chas Garland was sub-postmaster.

In 1978 Christine Pearce retired and Mrs Carole Hunt took over. Carole had already worked there for a couple of years and she was to become yet another long-serving sub-postmistress. Mr and Mrs Nordholm took over in 2000 and since 2003 it has been run by Chris & Jacqui Greenshields.

The Weavers: Back in the 1960s the Inglis family set out on a new venture. Lt Col Earnest John D'Oyly Inglis and his wife Angela moved from Truro to *Trefalghun* in 1960 and three years later they began trading as Mount Hawke Weavers; Mr Inglis had studied the subject at Falmouth Art School.

At its peak the business had eight or more looms ranging from a large flying shuttle, several Swedish type, to small tabletop looms. It produced a range of cotton and wool items: smocks with Old English *Rosepath* patterns, jackets, ponchos, bags…black cotton with bright patterns based on Greek designs…lengths of cloth for curtains, covers, bedspreads and rugs.

The goods were sold through their shop at *Trefalghun* and Mrs Inglis also travelled the country visiting potential customers with samples of their produce; this included taking bedspreads to Libertys in London.

Mr & Mrs Inglis, Liz Bennett (now Davies), Mrs Murrish and Edith Johns were the weavers and Mrs Stevens, Mrs Sprague, Mrs Murrish and Mrs Wilson some of the many ladies who undertook the sewing work. For a couple of years during the late 1960s a weaving outpost was set up in the Barbican at Penzance.

The business operated at *Trefalghun* until 1976 when Mrs Inglis died; it was then taken over by their daughter Jackie who ran it from Chapel Porth. The property then ceased to be used for commercial purposes and reverted to a dwelling.

Mr Inglis busy weaving

The Cobbler's Shop: John Andrew is the earliest boot and shoemaker that we have found; he appears in the Cornwall Trade Directories of 1856 and 1862. John Tregea was on the scene in 1878 and 1883 but it is Phil Jones who is best remembered in this role. His shop was in the old shed that still stands at the junction of the hill to Banns and the little road that leads down to the old corn mill at Trenithick.

We know quite a lot about Phil, through this letter from his son, Will Jones, who emigrated to America.

"My father, Philip Jones, was born in St Ives in 1865 and after learning a trade as a shoemaker, in Truro, he opened a shop in Mount Hawke in 1886. He chose there because it was close to the tin mines, he made heavy, hob-nail boots for the miners of St Agnes, St Day, Redruth and Camborne; many were also bought by local farmers.

He and his brother were near Navvy Pit or Wheal Music, digging out 'skimp-ing' for use in building our home. It stuck together when it was wet and they had to dig below it to get to the dry material. They must have dug too deep as it caved in on them. My uncle was killed and Dad received a broken hip which crippled him for the rest of his life. The house was in Banns Vale, called Philamaude (now Philamaud).

I was born in the house, on the 18th of April 1904, and went to school until the First World War began. Men and horses from the farms went off to war and my father had to make Army boots. Will Pearce was learning his trade with Dad at that time; he stayed with him for ten years.

I left school to work at Garland's Farm until 1918, when the war was over. The mines were laying people off at this time and I remember that some of the men came into my father's shop just to sit by the fire. Several retired gold min-ers returned from Mexico, India, Spain and Canada and they used to chat to us about their experiences.

My dad had a large garden and he loved it. He would come home for lunch and not go back to the shop until maybe 2.30 or 3.00 o'clock. We had to take his dinner to the shop at 5.30pm and he would work until 10.00pm which made it good for the old-timers, they had a place to sit and talk. I guess my dad didn't know what to do with me. He was a good father and wanted to keep me home. He bought 68 acres of good farmland, stocked it with four cows, pigs, a lovely horse, 100 chickens and told me to go to work.

It was about 1921 and there were quite a few young boys around and we started a football team. Our trainer was Harry Harper from St Agnes; he had just returned from Canada. His job was to look after the water works for St Agnes and Mount Hawke.

The Mount Hawke boys in the team were Harold Pearce, Roland Tonkin, Stanley Tonkin, Harry Tonkin, Gordon Snell, Harold Wilkins, P C Holman, Les Truan, Will Jolly, ? Hupton, Les White and Clarence Parsons. Harry Tonkin and I were the same age; we were pals.

We were all afraid of Gordon Snell's mother. He would often go home and tell her that we were rough with him and she would call the police, P C Benney. After that we would push Gordon around just to make her do it again. When P C Benney had gone we would tip over her water barrels. We played all sorts of tricks on people but not to hurt them. Often we would meet up in front of the chapel for a sing-song. If some strange fellow came after our girls we would put him in a wheelbarrow and dump him in the river or if he had a bicycle we would let the air out of his tyres.

The garden at Philamaude ran down to the mill; it was a busy place. It was owned and run by Walter Plumer; all the farmers had their corn crushed there. Walter and his mother lived in the cottage by the mill. The water to run it came from a mill pool at the bottom of Gover Hill. It was dammed at night and would run the mill waterwheel all the next day.

Les White and Clarance Parsons were the first of our bunch to leave the village... in 1921. At that time Henry Ford was advertising for young men to work in the new plant in Detroit making the Model T. The pay was 65 cents per hour, good money in the summer of 1923. Will Jose who had lived in Detroit for several years came home on holiday; his family lived in the house next to the railway halt. I think that it was he that persuaded me to go to the States."

In addition to his other problems Phil Jones also had the misfortune to lose an eye on a thorn while in his beloved garden.

Many people recall him working there and some still talk about the fun and games centred on his shop. Joan Chynoweth was happy to share her memories. "We used to go down there a lot. The soles of our shoes were leather and were forever wearing out. In the middle of the room was a little iron stove, Phil would be sitting behind it. The room was very untidy, full of cobwebs; he could never find people's shoes. There were seats but they were often taken, it was a favourite spot for the old men of the village like Cap'n Bill Harris and Henry Peters. They would go there to keep warm and to gossip. You could hardly breathe from pipe smoke."

Cap'n Bill Harris in the doorway, Will Jeffery with the dog and Phil Jones the cobbler at work in the early 1900s.

Chris Chynoweth recalled that the old men of the village had several gathering places including his father's carpentry workshop. He said, *"Unlike Phil Jones, my father didn't encourage them as they stopped him working. He didn't provide any seats so if they wanted to sit down they had to go over to the Institute or down to Jones' shop. In cold weather Jones lit his old cast iron stove and burnt offcuts of leather."*

Donald George recalled the other side of the story, the tricks that the lads from the village played on the cobbler and the old chaps around his stove. *"One of us would hold the door open with a stick while the other threw in some addled eggs or we'd put a tob on the chimney and jam the door closed with a broom handle. Phil Jones wasn't too pleased."*

The cobbler had a novel way of gaining revenge on the mischievous boys. He soaked bits of old leather in a bucket of water (there was no toilet in the building so the person who suggested that it might not have been clear water was probably correct). Phil referred to the resultant brew as his coffee and when one of the miscreants came into the shop he would dip a container into the stinking mixture and fling it over them with the retort, *"Have a cup ov coffee me ansome."*

Claude Tonkin recalled his mother, Dorothy Tonkin (née Jones), taking a jug of tea up the hill to him every afternoon; she was Phil's daughter. He also recalled Will Carlyon and Gordon Snell sitting in the shop talking to Phil Jones and just a while later placing tobs on the chimney. As Mary George reflected, *"It was all innocent fun by today's standards."*

In October 1937 the *St Austell Gazette* reported the death of Philip Jones, he had been a shoemaker for over 50 years.

Frederick G Docking had a cobbler's shop in Blackwater but worked at Mount Hawke on a part-time basis. He was certainly there in 1939 and it seems likely that he extended his business to there when Phil Jones died; his son, David Docking, thinks that he may have even used the same premises.

The old cobbler's shop survived long after its original purpose had become redundant; indeed it still exists but it no longer plays any role in the life of the village. It stands as a testament of a former age.

Will Jones' mentioned Will Pearce in his letter and it seems that he had his own cobblers' shop, in the little cottage next to what is now the florist's shop. (Shirley Barrett) His parents were butchers from Banns Vale.

The Barber's Shop: The old cobbler's took on another life when it became a hairdresser's shop. Harry Epplett worked from there and Monty Burrows recalled having his hair cut by him, *"Until he nearly took my ear off."* Michael Pheby also visited there but it was Harry Warren who cut his hair; he occasionally used it on Saturday mornings during the 1950s.

The Fish and Chip Shop: For three or four years during the very early 1950s (possibly earlier) the village could boast its own fish & chip shop. Olga and Len Grant ran it from a small building in Rope Walk, between the council houses and Peter Pollard's garage. Wesley George converted one of George Tallack's old coal stores and once the fryers were installed it must have looked the part. George Tallack was Olga's uncle. Within a few years, competition arrived when Monty Parsons started his mobile fish and chip service and the business closed. According to Shirley Barrett, Monty's venture was also short-lived; it ceased when his van caught fire. There was an even earlier fish and chip shop, in the 1920s a cone of chips was available from the cottage on the corner, later occupied by the Cowlings and Ted and Cicely Skimins.

Olga and Len in their Fish & Chip shop

The Bakery: Mr and Mrs William John (Jack) Cowling were the village bakers. From the memories of people who attended the school across the road we know that they were operating in the 1920s but it is possible that it was even earlier and from what Ted Skimins has told us they were there until 1962. They were aunt and uncle to Cicely Skimins, Ted's wife, who drove the baker's van.

The bakery was in a small building opposite the old school, where Ted's bungalow, *St Omer*, now stands. The Cowlings lived in the adjacent cottage, on the corner near the chapel. So many people have talked in glowing terms of the wonderful aroma that emanated from there that it sets the mouth watering even now.

The old bakery in the centre of photograph…taken from Carlyon's yard

Graham Carlyon has vivid memories of it; riding in the baker's van when Ted went out with pasties on the Saturday run to the pubs in the area and also of helping to make the doughnuts. He said, *"They had a special piece of equipment for making them and when you bit them the jam just oozed out."* I'll bet he tasted a few, as well.

According to Edith Johns the pasties were superb, *"They would even vary the contents to suit your taste; if you wanted one with less pepper or no onion it was no bother."*

Its closure as a bakery signalled the end of an era and with its passing went the evocative smell of bread and pasty recalled by so many former school children.

But that did not end the building's use, it continued life as Francis Garland's greengrocery store and then as Ted Skimins' barn up until its demolition sometime around 1990.

The baker's van

The Florists: Flowers by Diane is a few steps up the hill from the chapel, on the opposite side of the road. The building has a long and interesting history including carpentry, undertaking, engineering and possibly a few other uses. But in 1999 it was filled with the sweet smell of plants and flowers. Diane Lewis opened Flowers by Diane and was quickly accepted as part of the village scene with customers from far outside the village boundary.

Flowers by Diane

From Engineers to Craft Shop: The Collett family bought what is now the florists in 1973 and David and his father, Joe, commenced trading as Collett Engineering. Two years later they outgrew it and a larger workshop was built at the rear of the site. Miss Preen lived in the cottage next to the original workshop and when this became available in 1982 David and his father purchased it and redeveloped the entire front section to create a shop and a flat.

In 1985 David's brother, Stephen, purchased the premises and opened a new business, Colletts Hardwood and Woodwork Supplies. Their father, Joe, was also involved in this venture. The front area became a craft shop and the rear section a joinery workshop.

The Tailor: Richard John Menadue was a tailor and appears as such in the 1878 to 1910 trade directories. He lived in a cottage in a row that once stood on the site of The Village Stores (this was Neddie Mewton's butcher's shop) facing a field where the bungalow *Greenacres* has been built. Richard also ran a Dame school and it is possible that both his tailoring and teaching took place at this location. He was also the Church Parish Clerk at the time of the building of the new church; he died in 1917, aged 85. His daughter was Mary Chynoweth (née Menadue), the village sub-postmistress for many years. She was the mother of Harry, the village carpenter and undertaker, and grandmother of Joan and Chris Chynoweth.

Mr & Mrs Richard John Menadue

The Blacksmith: According to the Harrods' Trade Directory, Simon Coleman was the Mount Hawke blacksmith in 1878 and in 1887 and 1902 it was Edwin Coleman, presumably a relation. The directory includes outlying areas but in most cases they are identified and as there is no such reference here we assume that the Colemans were based within the village.

Circa 1905 ... The blacksmith's shop on the right of the road

Edgar Rodda (b 1887) is listed between the years 1910 to 1933; he operated from the blacksmith's shop which once stood at the front of *Greenacres,* next to where The Village Stores now stands. He married Evelyne Davey but died aged only 48, in 1935. Evelyne later re-married and became Mrs Miners.

Edgar Rodda probably taken around 1930

Harold Wilkins (b. 1902) was apprenticed to Edgar Rodda, from 1917 to about 1922. He then worked for Mitchell Brothers at Bridge before running his own blacksmith business at Wheal Rose. When he retired he moved his forge to his back garden at *Trevone* and continued to do odd jobs well into the 1970s.

Edgar Rodda holding the horse with apprentice Harold Wilkins beside him…on the left of the photograph is Charlie Harris

Joan Chynoweth recalled the old blacksmith's shop in the 1920s which she described as, *"Two old cottages, one where Mr Rodda had his anvil and fire and the other which had no roof and was just a yard enclosed by walls. It was a lovely sight to see the big shire horses with their leather harness and gleaming horse brasses. We would watch him in the yard gripping the horse's hoof and prising off the old shoe. We would ask if it hurt and then go into the forge to watch him hammering away at the new shoe on the anvil."*

Following Edgar's death his son, Monty Rodda, took over the business. Monty was born in 1914 and worked with his father for some years; in 1935 he became the blacksmith. He married Phyllis Roach in 1937 and they lived at *Phylmont* (now *Chy-lehan*) and farmed the surrounding land. This was across the road from *Trelawney,* in the field behind Joan Chynoweth's bungalow. The cows were hand-milked in a shed next to their new home, the milk poured from buckets into churns, cooled and placed on the stand by the road. Like most farmers of that time they also kept pigs and poultry.

Monty continued his smithy work for some years but the world was becoming less reliant on genuine horsepower and demand for the services of the farrier and the smith gradually reduced. The business worked in conjunction with his farm and it is difficult to give an actual date when he last fired-up the forge; perhaps the late 1940s or even the early 1950s.

Monty and Phyllis moved from *Phylmont* to a cottage down the road for a few years and in 1954 they built another bungalow, *Greenacres,* it was here that they later ran a social club. For a few years the blacksmith's shop stood empty and sometime around 1959 or 1960 it was demolished. Monty was living at *The Elms* when in 1965 he died, aged just 51.

The Builders, Carpenters & Undertakers … so many of them:

A little further up the road from the smithy, opposite *The Elms,* was Ernest Rodda's workshop from where he ran his carpentry and undertaking business, probably from the turn of the century until about 1916. Ernest was born in 1880, almost certainly in *Menagissey Vean.*

Mary Rodda, Ernest's daughter, thinks that her grandfather, Richard Rodda (d. 1919), was also a carpenter and probably used the same workshop. This seems likely as there was a Richard John Rodda, carpenter, in trade directories between the dates of 1878 to 1906. By 1910 his name had disappeared, replaced by Ernest Rodda.

In 1916 Ernest married Mildred Annie Santo from St Agnes and they started farming at Wheal Rose, Mary was born four years later. He was very involved in public life and served on the Parish, District and County Councils.

Circa 1915…a wheelwright at work outside the carpenter's shop in the main street

In 1939 Mary moved to live at *Westwood* in Menagissey and began her long involvement with the Mount Hawke Church and the Women's Institute.

Mary said, *"John Rodda, my great grandfather, was also a Mount Hawke man, he lived in Spry Cottage which is in Rope Walk, just below where the council houses were built.*

Edgar the blacksmith and my father were brothers. The family owned the land between their two workshops, from the main street back to what is now Rodda's Road. It was eventually sold to Bill Jolly who built bungalows there."

Jack May of *Beacon View* was a carpenter and painter but from the invoices to Mrs Johns of *The Laurels*, the cottage adjoining *Henly House*, it was clear that he carried out all sorts of general building work. One item was for fixing launders, Cornish for roof gutters.

The charges for his time are an interesting piece of social history. In June 1937 he worked for 10d an hour, that's just over 4p. By October 1939, that's two and a half years later, his rate had increased by five percent, to 10½d. It had gone up to two shillings and three pence an hour (11.25p) by 1950; the percentage increase for this I will leave to those more proficient at compound interest calculations.

While Jack was busy with his building work his wife, Winnie, George Tallack's sister, was running their hardware shop. Their grandson, Rodney Grant, recalled the little shop in Rope Walk, opposite the old fish and chip shop, where they sold paint, wallpaper, galvanised iron sheets, general hardware, paraffin and mentholated spirits. It seems that it closed in the early 1950s. Rodney Grant continues the family tradition as he operates his decorating business from his home in the main street.

The florist's shop has had a varied past; a part of the property was for many years Richard Jenkins' carpentry workshop; he is listed in the trade directories of 1856 to 1902, sometimes as Jenkin and in other entries as Jenkins.

He was Lorna White's great-grandfather and in addition to being a carpenter he also farmed at Croft Prince Farm and is listed as such in the 1897 Kelly's Directory. Lorna's son, Ross White, now farms there.

Harry Chynoweth, known to most people as Cap'n Har, later took over the workshop and ran his business from there. He was born in America in 1884 and came to this country while an infant. He served his apprenticeship with Matthew Hodge at St Agnes before going back to the USA in 1902, at the age of 18. He returned in 1918 and set up his business. In 1920 he married Evelyn Gilchrist and they had two children…Joan and Chris, both still live in the village.

Joan Chynoweth was born in 1922, at 2 Alexandra Terrace, but three years later the family moved to a new bungalow, *Sunnymeade*, built by Harry and her grandfather, George Gilchrist who was born near Navvy Pit. George lived in Blackwater, in the house where it is suggested John Passmore Edwards was born.

Joan recalled the workshop as her favourite place, *"I loved to watch my father working there. It was right in the centre of the village, the remains of a row of old cottages. It had an earth floor and you were always ankle deep in wood shavings and I liked the rustling sound as I walked about. I know it's a bit gruesome but I used to watch him making a coffin and putting in the pillows and lining."*

Chris Chynoweth also has fond memories of his father working there except one occasion when he and his mates were caught red-handed when Harry returned to fetch something. They had let themselves in to explore and his father was none too happy. Chris said, *"The place had a beaten earth floor and an upstairs office. My father made the coffins and sometimes I helped him."*

It seems that Harry managed to run his business without the use of a telephone and I suppose that those who are plagued by the thing can imagine the time that he must have saved. To book a hearse he would send a postcard to Williams of Redruth asking them to be there at the particular time. On one occasion it failed to turn up and, with everyone standing around waiting, Harry hurried down to the phone-box. There were a few silent moments on the line until he was told that it would be there in ten minutes. The hearse duly arrived and Harry accepted that the delay was caused by a puncture. The next time that he bumped into Mr Williams he said, *"Here, you gave me some cock and bull story about that puncture. I knew it wasn't true when I found the postcard in my back pocket."*

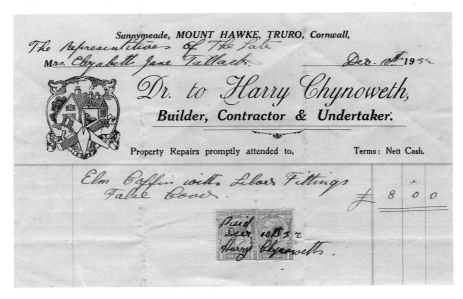

Harry Chynoweth's invoice for a funeral

Following Harry's death in 1958 local builder Bill Jolly used the building as a workshop for his work around the village.

Des White trained as a cabinetmaker. He came to Mount Hawke in 1950 and at first he split his time between carpentry and working on his father-in-law's farm. In 1952 he built a bungalow, *Boscavene*, at Croft Prince, near a thatched cottage where he and his wife, Lorna (née Jose), were then living.

During the late 1950s he had a slight change of direction as he began his long career as an undertaker; he built a chapel of rest near their home and the business steadily grew. He became involved in public life and served on the Parish and District Councils and was also a school manager. When he died, in 2002, Lorna converted the chapel into a bungalow and called it *Chy Gwyn* (White House).

Douglas Stephens' little joinery workshop was on the hill down to Banns, a little way up the lane next to where the bottom shop once offered its wares. His store was in the old cobbler's shop. Despite its limited size this little building later became Archie Pheby's carpenter's shop, from about 1960 to 1979. Archie's younger son, Alan, worked for him and eventually took over the business leaving him to enjoy a long retirement. He died in 2007, aged 94.

After the woodworking tools had been cleared away Michael Pheby used the building as a store for a while until Mark Hambridge took it over.

The old shed today with Archie's board still over the door

The Greengrocer: There was a time when most people grew their own vegetables but after the Second World War the fruit and veg man began to call. Raphael Thomas arrived at all hours of the night and Donald George said, *"It was no wonder, he used to watch Match of the Day at Jimmy Green's and then set out to finish his round."*

Sharman Burrows recalled Raphael calling on her Gran so late that the door had to left unlocked and a bowl placed out for the vegetables. Edith Johns said that he acquired the nickname of the *Midnight Greengrocer*.

Francis Garland was more into wholesale greengrocery and used the old bakery building as a store.

The Coalman: It would appear that from a young age George Tallack helped in the family business delivering coal and corn around the area. He had lost his sight when he developed diabetes while a teenager but that didn't stop him working and later running the business.

Circa 1900…George Tallack with a cartload of coal in Ropewalk

Claude Tonkin drove a lorry for Will James of Porthtowan during the mid 1940s and recalled the regular requests to collect a load of coal from St Agnes Station. He said, *"George was a powerful man but you had to make sure he was facing in the right direction or else the coal went all over the place. If you stood too close he'd have your head off with his shovel. I've seen him drive it into* the wooden sideboards so far that it was difficult to get out. We'd take the load back to his place at the end of Rope Walk ... where Peter Pollard's garage is now. I had to tip the coal into his shed where he would weigh it on his scales. That sounds a bit difficult for a blind man but he managed it. He then bagged it up and stacked it three deep and did as neat a job as anyone who could see." George also stored coal in the little building nearby which later became the fish and chip shop.

For deliveries around the village he used a hand-cart and was often guided by a friend but if it was further out it was taken by lorry. Claude said, "We were delivering down at Banns, by the river. I stopped the lorry and asked George where we had to take it. He said, 'Follow me' which sounds alright until you consider that he was totally blind. We had some bags to drop off for Sammy Blitchford and his mother, up at Splat. George said, 'Right Claude, take a bag and see if you can get in.' I reached the door and Sammy's mother came out and said, 'George will bring it in thank you.' George reckoned that they had an earth floor and didn't want anyone to see it ... that was no problem with George, of course."

Claude Tonkin with Will James' lorry

George sang in the chapel choir, wrote music and could often be heard beating time on the back of the pew. Christine Pearce recalled that her husband, Claude, was a friend of his and that if they were out in the fog, George could always find his way home.

John Jotcham told the story of a chapel meeting when the Reverend White raised the question of finance for the Manse and George said, *"That's all very well Reverend but the Manse is looking like Buckingham Palace while the chapels are like the stables what b'long to 'n."* George Tallack died in 1956 aged 73.

Before George Tallack came on the scene, coal was hauled from the station to the village in carts. It was in large blocks, perhaps three feet across, and had to be broken before it could be used.

Circa 1910... Howard Chynoweth (in black coat) with George Tallack

Garages & Motor Sales: Almost opposite the post office, just about where Graham and Rita Carlyon now have their entrance gate, was a shed. Will Carlyon bought it from Harry Chynoweth and rented it to Douglas Stephens who operated his motorbike business from there during the 1950s. Douglas also had the old cobbler's shop, a little further down the hill, and it is possible that he began selling from there. After a while he sold cars from the old Nissen hut at the top of Roddas Road (Back Lane); a building erected in 1948 as an implement shed for *Carn View Farm.*

The garage circa 1956

The building with a large forecourt, on the approach road into the village, became known to a generation as *George and Stephens Garage*. Donald George built the first section in 1956 and began his car repairs and petrol sales business. In 1963 he enlarged it to provide space for car sales and Douglas Stephens transferred his activities there.

Douglas died in 1970 and two years later Donald decided to retire; he sold the premises to Kingsley Mills. Since then the property has passed through a number of hands and been put to a variety of uses including clothing manufacturing, furniture storage, marine leisure, second-hand furniture sales and now a shop, WHYY.

The garage after it had been extended in 1963

Peter Pollard opened his car repairs garage in 1982 at the top end of Rope Walk, in what had once been George Tallack's old coal store. It sits adjacent to *Ropers Walk Farm* where Peter and his wife Elizabeth raise a few cattle and provide holiday accommodation.

Haulage: George Arnold Carlyon was one of three brothers who ran haulage and threshing businesses; their father, Charlie Carlyon, also worked with steam engines. George Arnold and Ada Carlyon (née Sampson) lived in Mount Hawke, at *Trefalghun House,* where their children William (b. 1911) and Iris (b. 1913, later Mrs Climas) were born. The family then moved across the road to *Pendeen* where there was more space to develop the business. That must have been just prior to 1914 because their third child, Kay (later Mrs Caddy), was born there.

George Arnold Carlyon's steam engines were a regular sight towing their large trailers, collecting coal for the mines or sand for the fields. The sand came from Gwithian, three wagons were taken there and while the first two were being delivered the last one was being filled. Graham Carlyon recalled their three steam engines, *Millennium King* (a name and nameplate later adopted by Neddie Mewton), *Lorna Doone* and *Pissy Belly*. The latter was not the real name but was given because it was always leaking water, the real name may well have been *Her Majesty*.

George also had threshing sets and his account book included an item in 1928 when the charge for a traction engine, threshing set and two men for three-quarters of a day was the princely sum of £2.17.6 (about £2.88). Towards the end of his time in the business he became involved in general haulage and bought two non-tipping lorries, a Liberty and a Pearce Arrow/ Peerless...both ex First World War vehicles. Claude Tonkin recalled playing in them during the mid 1930s, when they had ceased to be used in the business. Will Carlyon once told him that one of them was later cut up and used as a trailer.

George Carlyon in the centre of the picture beside his ex First World War lorry overseeing the delivering of a railway carriage to Carn Brea in the early 1920s

Gordon Snell worked one of the traction engines at the quarry at Menagissey, breaking stone for roadwork; he also helped with threshing at local farms. The crushing work at the quarry was later taken over by a gas driven crusher. (Shirley Barrett)

George Arnold Carlyon died in 1937, he was only in his 50s, and his son, William Arnold Carlyon, then took over. By this time the business was concentrating on general haulage.

Will married Sylvia Dibbs and they had two children, Graham and Sharman; both still live in the village. Tragically Sylvia died in the mid 1950s, aged only forty.

There was a tragic accident at the quarry; Harry Bawden was crushed to death when the ground collapsed on him. Will Carlyon had just paid the men and was climbing out of the quarry; he looked back and saw the ground moving. He shouted a warning and everyone ran but Harry was trapped by the fall. Shortly after the quarry closed.

Circa 1960... Carlyon's driver Claude Tonkin took this photograph of early lorries at Hayle. Drivers left to right are Gordon Snell, Raymond Tippett & Cecil Jose.

During Will Carlyon's time Cornwall County Council became their main customer and the firm grew to include six or seven lorries, a loader and a tracked machine...a considerable business.

Claude Tonkin said, *"When I was a boy I often rode down to the quarry in George Carlyon's green Humber car and while he was with the men I played on* an old steam engine which had been dumped in the lane. And then, in 1954, I started working for them; I was there for 35 years. When I started the wage was £7.5.0 (£7.25) for a five and a half day week."

Claude's wife, Betty, interrupted, "You were meant to finish at midday on Saturday but by the time you arrived home half the afternoon was gone. He always had to clean his lorry, it was his pride and joy."

Claude continued, "At first I drove a Bedford four cubic yard tipper but in 1965 they bought a new Thames Trader… BCV 54C. I was the only one to drive it but eventually it was replaced with a larger vehicle. It was always my favourite; they never sold it and it's still used for rallies.

It was a good place to work; I remember Leonard Kemp struggling to fill the grease gun, no sooner was his back turned than Cecil Jose would grab it. He wasn't too pleased."

Claude Tonkin with his beloved Thames Trader at a rally

Graham Carlyon said, "Any slack time was spent in making concrete blocks; I hated that job. The fuel pump was next to the Men's Institute, near where we washed the lorries. *Local farmer Ted Skimins often walked by and for some reason the hose would be accidentally directed across the road. On one occasion he was out for revenge and managed to throw a full bucket of water over me; I was soaked. I filled a bucket and coosed (chased) after him. He begged for mercy but he had the lot."*

By the early 1960s Graham was working in the business and when his father died in the late 1970s he took over and ran it with the help of his wife, Rita. Although Cornwall County Council had reduced their reliance on outside contractors there was sufficient work to maintain and even grow the business; it currently has eight lorries and a number of excavators.

When the American manufacturer Michigan produced an international calendar of their products the Carlyon's machine was used for the British entry.

Graham and Rita Carlyon with members of staff in 1992… (L to R) Stephen Beard, Arthur James, Rita Carlyon, Graham Carlyon, Claude Tonkin, Graham Green, David Thomas, Kenny Porter & Frankie Richards

Some of Carlyon's fleet of lorries in 2003/04 with drivers (L to R) Kenny Porter, Frankie Richards, Clifford Goss & Will Medlyn (Photo Martin Caddy)

Some of the staff at G A Carlyon's: Gordon Snell (42 years), Ewart Tippett, Raymond Tippett from Blackwater (30 years), Bert Hocking, Clarence Littlejohn from St Day, Alfie Richards, David Hall (1968-1985), Donald Thomas, Leonard Kemp, Claude Tonkin (35 years), Cecil Jose (32 years) and many more.

Public Houses and Hotels:

Les Douch of the Cornwall Museum prepared a list of licensed premises in the St Agnes Parish, there is just one entry for Mount Hawke, the Miner's Arms 22nd July 1836. Even then, this almost certainly referred to the one at Towan Cross.

Henry Libby held the licence for the Red Lion in 1856 but it closed in 1863. According to Frank Carpenter in the St Agnes Museum Trust Journal, it was situated behind the current post office. A contemporary newspaper said, *"The Methodists of Mount Hawke starved the publican out."*

Lorna White recalled being told of a kiddleywink in the middle cottage of the row that runs back from the existing post office but this may have been the Red Lion. *Old Oak Cottage* was said to have been a drinking house and the Women's Institute scrapbook refers to another at Manor Parsley, in the valley towards Navvy Pit. They existed in most communities and it is suggested that there were ten or eleven in the district. But then they disappeared. By 1863 there was not an inn left in Mount Hawke. The coming of the teetotal movement, introduced by Joseph Livesey in the North of England and miners returning from America, spread throughout Cornwall. At first there was opposition to the movement but it gained strength and innkeepers found it safer to close their doors.

The *Pent-y-Bryn* was an attractive house positioned facing the Short Cross road junction. It was built as a dwelling but later it became a guesthouse and, at the time of its demise, a pub.

Peter Wilkins said his father remembered it being built, with stone from *Prince Croft Farm* quarry. This was in 1908 or maybe a little later; it certainly could not have been earlier as it does not appear on the 1907 Ordnance Survey map.

It was built for Mrs Collins who, according to Shirley Barrett, moved there in 1911; that was when she purchased her furniture from Criddle & Smith of Truro. In her younger days she had been a bal maid at Tywarhayle Mine.

In 1918 Charlie Welden rented it and lived there with one of his daughters; a year later they purchased it. Another daughter married into the Garland family, they were Francis's parents.

Captain Basil James Ohlson DSO moved there in the late 1920s; his son, Douglas Hereward Ohlson, then lived there.

Many other names have been associated with the property including The Reverend Donald Forway whose parents owned it during the 1940s. Donald said, *"Pent-y-Bryn is a Welsh name meaning property or house on the hill. We called it Penty-Bryn but I feel that Pent-y-Bryn is correct. We bought it in 1943 or 1944, I was about 16 and my brother was 12 and we moved in before our parents who were still involved in selling their business in London. It was important to occupy the house as empty property was being commandeered by the military."*

Local businessman Ivey Mollard lived there during the late 1940s and 1950s, they were followed by Mr and Mrs H W Mulvey who ran it as a Fully Licensed Free House. The conversion to this new use was recorded in the Women's Institute scrapbook as *"The end of a century in the dry."* Advertised as, *"Picturesque, spacious, fronted by Sun Lounges and extensive lawns in a superb setting,"* the property had a large car park and a walled garden.

The Pent-y-Bryn as a private hotel

This internal view of Pent-y-Bryn was from the 1970s when Des and Rita Solomon ran it as a free house...they built a reputation for superb entertainment and good food. It was extremely successful and attracted a clientele from a wide area

The Mills family purchased the property and continued to run it as a public house for about two years but on a hot September afternoon in 1978, disaster struck. Carl Mills said, *"We had carried out a lot of refurbishment but our efforts went up in smoke when an electrical fault caused a major fire and the building was destroyed. Our immediate intention was to re-build it but the Planning Authority were insistent on sticking to the original design; the cost would have been prohibitive."* The site was cleared and in the early 1980s the spacious grounds were developed into a small complex of bungalows and houses.

Monty Rodda had been a blacksmith and farmer but in the late 1950s he and his wife, Phyllis, decided it was time for a complete change of career, they opened a club… *The Spider's Web.* The old blacksmith's shop, which had stood on the edge of the main road through the village for so many years, was demolished and the lounge of their bungalow, *Greenacres*, was converted into a bar. This must have been a controversial move in this village with no pub and even now the venture is talked about as being a bit before its time.

The club was said to be *for the social intercourse of ladies and gentlemen and the provision of opportunities for rational recreation and refreshment as well as to afford the members facilities for meeting one another and entertaining their friends.* The proprietor was John Edgar Montague Rodda of Mount Hawke but it had a properly constituted committee with a subscription of 5/- (25p) for Ordinary Members but temporary membership was available at 2/6.

Diana Rodda was very young at the time but can recall many of the customers who used it. Graham Carlyon said that even though some boys were too young to be members they could often buy a drink, served through one of the rear windows.

The business ran for only a couple of years and during that time it seemed to attract quite a lot of interest from the licensing authority. Its final demise followed a raid; it was at a time when late drinking often meant the loss of the licence. Monty and Phyllis were still awaiting their formal licence so the late session was probably a tad unwise.

Their daughter, Ann, recalled that a policeman asked why they were still serving drinks and Monty tried to explain it away by saying that they were celebrating her degree. Phyllis, by this time, was feverishly collecting glasses and pouring the contents down the sink. The policeman turned to one lady and asked what she was drinking. Clearly unaware of the implications she replied, *"I'll have a gin and lime please."* That did it, the licence was a forlorn hope and the club closed. It had lasted only a year or two. Monty and Phyllis were devastated, they had poured all of their energies into the project and it had fallen at the first hurdle.

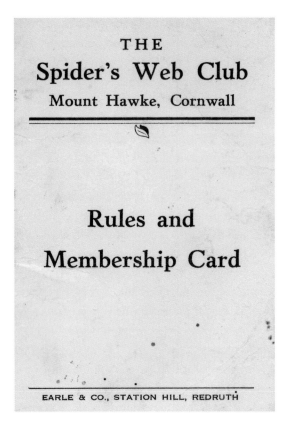

THE
Spider's Web Club
Mount Hawke, Cornwall

Rules and

Membership Card

EARLE & CO., STATION HILL, REDRUTH

The Spider's Web Club... Rules and membership Card (Courtesy of John Hilton)

THE SPIDER'S WEB CLUB
MOUNT HAWKE - CORNWALL

Member's Name *Mr & Mrs Cockle*

Address *Prince Royal Meadow*

M't Hawke Truro

Membership No. *169 & 170*

Mr and Mrs Cockle's membership card (Courtesy of John Hilton)

Following the fire at the Pent-y-Bryn the village was without a pub again and the road to the Victory Inn at Towan Cross must have been well trodden. It is strange that the construction of a new school should have changed the situation but the redundant 1874 building was considered ideal for a licensed premises and in 1988 Ron and Jan Dawson opened a new public house, *The Old School*. The hunt was on for the oldest ex-pupil to perform the launch and, accompanied by the St Agnes Town Crier and Caharrack & St Day Silver Band, Gordon Snell pulled the first pint.

In November 1992 Matthew Bond wrote in The Packet newspaper, *"Mount Hawke, once a haven for tee-totallers, is now a proper village... the building of a pub has assured that. Seen as a blessing by some and unnecessary by a few others, the pub stands tall in the old school building and looks very apt in its surroundings."*

The *Old School* was not the first licensed premises since the days when the village was dry but who could blame him for using a bit of creative journalism to welcome the new village amenity.

Ian and Rose Davies succeeded the Dawsons and remained there until 2008.

The *Old School* in 2008

Glen View was a four-bedroom cottage on the road down to Banns and in 1971 it was up for sale. The Hutton family were then living at *Tregarthen* (now *Trevellyan*) next to the post office where they offered Bed and Breakfast accommodation but Mavis Hutton had taken a fancy to *Glen View* and suggested to Clive that they should make an offer. His response? *"Oh no, not again."* But what chance do mere men stand in such matters; the offer was made and it was theirs.

Mavis said, *"Archie Pheby added three bedrooms and carried out a lot of other work but there were all sorts of problems in getting it finished. Until, that is, some friends intervened. 'Right,' they said, ' you're moving in today.' The builders were a bit surprised and so were our Bed and Breakfast guests who arrived back from a day out to find that we'd moved. They had to transfer down the road to our new property. Strange really, they never came back to stay with us again. We transferred the name from our old cottage and Glen View became Tregarthen."*

In 1991 there was an important milestone, they received an award from the Automobile Association for being placed in the top twenty one-star hotels in the country. When the time came to close, Mavis and Clive had run the hotel for almost 30 years.

Tregarthen Guest House

Ernest Cocking was offering apartments to rent at *Glen View* in the 1930s where *attendance and board residence with bath was available.* Mrs Florence A Harris had accommodation at *Sunny Ridge* in 1935 and in the

1964/65 Official Porthtowan Guide there were Holiday Bungalows at Anderson's Chalets, Mount Hawke, Truro.

The Ropemaker: The Hawke family once made ropes in the village and the area where they are said to have lived and worked is still known as Rope-walk. It is supposed that the business flourished in the 18th century, in line with the demands of the mines. (A ropewalk is described in the Wikipedia on-line encyclopedia as a long straight narrow lane, or a covered pathway, where long strands of material were laid before being twisted into rope) It doesn't take too much imagination to picture the activity in this road. No doubt the weather was always good. In an audio recording Will Jones suggests that Rope Walk was also referred to as The Lane.

Doctors Surgery: Mount Hawke was well served by the doctors at St Agnes but the huge growth in housing meant that the village needed its own surgery. The brand new building was opened in August 1983 and it is now difficult to imagine life without it.

Henly Residential Home: For many years the private residence of the Garland family, it was converted into a residential home with a purpose-built extension at the rear. It closed in 2001 and was redeveloped as housing.

Circa 1910… A Mount Hawke street scene with Henly House on the left

The Sandman: Not the man who sends you to sleep but the one who delivers the sand to dress your floors; an old practice common to all villages. It was delivered to the home for the housewife to spread over her freshly scrubbed kitchen floor to soak up any spillages. It was eventually brushed up and discarded.

Charlie Harris (Charlie Ham), with his donkey and cart, was the main supplier for the area; he carried it from St Agnes Beacon and sold a full pail for a few pence. *"Mrs Mutton remembered the special cupboard in which her great grandmother kept her sand… A special greyish/white sand, taken from a mound to the north of Navvy Pit, was used for scrubbing tables."* (W I 1950)

Charlie travelled to Redruth every Friday to collect newspapers and other items for the villagers but on the 2nd February 1916 he made the news, *"Mr Charles Harris of Mount Hawke, whilst attending Redruth Market on Friday, was seized with apoplexy and died early on Saturday morning. For nearly 30 years he had been a visitor to the market. He was blind and his ability to get about was the wonder of all. Mount Hawke Wesleyan Church, by his death, loses a devoted member and local preacher."*

Charlie Harris with his delivery cart and pair of donkeys… his wife and daughter are in the doorway

Accumulators: During the 1920s Ernest Mitchell ran an accumulator charging business from his little shed down the lane by *The Elms*. Many years later, in the 1950s, it was Edgar Carter who provided this service, when he was not driving one of his buses. He operated from a little wooden shed in the bus yard, in Rope Walk. He was also a Radio Ham and made crystal sets; Monty Burrows remembered buying one from him.

Taxi Service: We have already mentioned a number of people who provided taxi services in the village and to this list must be added Stanley Stevens who, in the 1940s, took over an existing business from Monty Parsons. Stanley lived in the cottage next to the shop in the square and when he died, in 1965, his wife, Connie Stevens (née Parsons), continued to run it. A regular run was to transport children from Mawla, Nancekuke and Porthtowan, to and from Mount Hawke School. Connie still lives in the village and, together with her daughter Vivienne Honey and granddaughter Emma Thomas, was able to provide us with some useful information. Monty Rodda also ran a limited taxi service with a few regular customers.

Vivienne Stevens in the mid 1960s beside the family taxi

Ice-Cream: Edgar Vincent was an ice-cream man, certainly during the 1930s and perhaps earlier. Donald George recalled, *"You could buy a ½d cornet in those days and if you hung around long enough he'd top it up for you. He travelled around with a little ice cream cart pulled by a pony."*

His son-in-law, Monty Parsons, took over the business and he and his wife, Chrissie, spent hours selling ice-cream from a number of locations including Porthtowan Beach. Sharman Burrows said, *"Chrissie worked really hard and wouldn't leave until the last person was off the beach."*

Claude Tonkin was a young lad in the 1930s; at a time before small suppliers had any form of refrigeration. He said that they made as much as they needed for the day and you could go there at the end of his round and he would fill your bowl; you could eat as much as you wanted for a few coppers.

Parson's ice cream van on Porthtowan Beach

Skips for Hire: In times past rubble and rubbish was cleared by horse and cart…shovelled in and shovelled out. This gave way to small lorries which progressively increased in size across the years. A feature of the modern Construction Industry, and of the DIY enthusiast, is skip hire of the type provided by Craig Hutton, through his business, Skip-It. With containers of varying size Craig is a familiar sight as he transports all sorts of unwanted material to the tip.

A puzzle: The Original Jig-Saw Puzzle Club is listed in trade directories from 1923 to 1939. It took us a while to resolve this one but we eventually found that it was Ashley Rowe who manufactured them, in his wooden shed near the railway halt. He sold them all over the country. Mrs Rowe also rented them out and if one was returned with a piece missing her husband made a replacement.

Mangle Houses: Those families who could afford it took their washing to a mangle house where the water would be squeezed out of the wet clothes and bed linen; there were at least two such houses in Mount Hawke. One was a little way up the hill from *Trefalghan* and, according to Chris Chynoweth, the other was in the row of cottages on the site of what is now, The Village Stores (Neddie Mewton's butcher's shop). According to the Women's Institute scrapbook the old fashioned mangles were about ten feet long with rollers weighed down by stones.

Mrs Whitford and another lady on their way to the mangle house in one of the three cottages on the right

Upholstery: Len Grant was an upholsterer. He transferred his business from the Camborne/Redruth area to Mount Hawke in 1968 and established it in a pre-fabricated building in Rope Walk; he retired in the late 1980s.

Photographer: We have come across a number of 1950s photographs by John B Hewitson who advertised as *Portrait and General Photographer;* you could ring him by dialling Porthtowan 56.

Other Businesses & Services:

The 1922 Christmas souvenir booklet produced by the Mount Hawke Wesley Society to raise funds for the heating and lighting fund includes a number of trade notices, some relate to local people. M M Rowe of Mount Hawke Stores offered cakes and chocolates with iced cakes made to order. Also on offer was a circulating library, china, stationery and postcards of the neighbourhood. Richard John (Jack) Pearce of Manor Parsley was a butcher, perhaps one of many; he was still mentioned in the trade directory in 1939. He claimed to be the oldest established business of its kind in the parish with the slogan *Buy of the one who treats you the best, who chooses the best beasts and rejects all the rest.* He sold his meat out of an old butcher's wagon. There was competition from J H Vellenoweth from Beacon, St Agnes, (known as *the shop on wheels*) who travelled to Mount Hawke to offer his *Prime ox and heifer beef, English lamb and dairy fed pork.*

Connie Stevens recalled her aunt, Eliza Richards, who sold meat during the late 1800s and early 1900s. Her house was just up the hill from the chapel, next to where the Mary Chynoweth (née Menadue) had her post office. One window faced the street and it was through this opening that Eliza served her customers. Connie said that the house then stood empty for a while before Harry Chynoweth renovated it and Miss Boskeen lived there.

Circa 1910...To the right of the post office is the house from where Mrs Richards sold meat

Mr J C Pearce invited those on holiday to visit his utility prize poultry farm and aviary for stock and song birds and W C Pearce was a *Practical shoemaker* who would make and repair your shoes.

The fish came from Chacewater, well at least that's where the fishman lived! During the early 1940s Mr Bryant toured the villages with his pony and wagon selling his seafood.

John Goyne offered conveyancy and estate agency work at Mount Hawke House and had a trade directory listing in 1878 and 1883. It seems likely that it was the same John Goyne who undertook accountancy work in the 1880s.

Thomas Worley Noble was a sheet metal worker in the 1930s; he worked from the long building just below the chapel. George Williams from Blackwater was a mobile grocer in the 1950s and 1960s. Albert Jose, mason and decorator, lived at Manor Parsley, Manny Cockle, decorator, was from Banns; Rodney Grant was apprenticed to him. Eric Thorne ran his Vac-hospital from the 1970s to the 1990s, out near the railway halt, and Pat Sheffield ran a pet shop next to the grocer's in the square. Upstairs was the hairdressers, firstly Sharon Stevens, then Tracy Thomas and since about 2000, Jenny Gibson who operates as Hairlines Unisex Hairdressing Salon.

The St Agnes Parish Jubilee Souvenir Programme included only three trade advertisements for Mount Hawke: J H D White (Funeral Director),

Rod Grant (Painter Decorator Signwriter) of *Shenfield*, Mount Hawke, and Alan Green of Trenethick Dairy.

There are many gardens to be tended in the village … homes of retired folk or working families. Phillip Borlase or Diana Rodda are on hand with their horticulture businesses.

Circa 1910 … Yet another butcher
T E Matthews of Chacewater with his meat van in The Yard at the end of Rope Walk

Mount Hawke boasts many other business, both past and present. We have made no attempt to produce a comprehensive list; those mentioned have been collected along the way. We hope that they give a flavour of this self-supporting community. If your favourite business has not appeared in this section then it has been missed and we apologise for that. But if it relates to farming, mining and transport then read on … these were considered so important to the area that they have been included as dedicated chapters.

Farming

According to Robert Symons in the *West Briton* of the 23rd November 1876, much of the land between Blackwater and Mount Hawke in 1840 was unenclosed. The *Gazatteer of Cornwall* suggests that there was little change by 1884 when it recorded that fifty percent of the land in the parish of St Agnes was open downs covered with gorse and heather. Small wonder that much of the farmer's time was spent in reclamation work; many thousands of tons of beach sand and seaweed were transported inland and used as dressing.

The Women's Institute scrapbook asserts that farming was on a much smaller scale in those days with much of the land unfenced common. It states, "*On the slopes however, fields were cut out to grow corn, this was ground at the local mills and the straw used for thatching.*" Of course, much of the area was used for mining and now lies derelict.

There were a number of local corn mills including the imposing building which still exists in the valley between Gover and Banns, sometimes referred to as Gover or Tywarnhayle Mill but probably better known as Trenithick Mill after the area in which it stands. The Women's Institute scrapbook states, "*The great wheel was made at St Agnes Quay and drawn thence by a team of five horses owned and led by Mr Thomas.*" William Plummer operated it in 1878; Mrs Maria Plummer and her son, Walter, ran it from 1883 to 1923.

The machinery was driven by a waterwheel, taking its power from the water of the mill pool at the bottom of Gover Hill. The pool was dammed at night and released down the leat when needed. Bags of corn were brought there by local farmers on wagons or carts and hoisted to the loft by a pulley. The bags were pulled through the trap doors which then closed behind them.

Circa 1900 ... Looking across the valley towards Trenithick Mill

Circa 1905 ... Mrs Plummer and her son Walter outside Trenithick Mill

Francis Matthews was blind but that didn't stop him operating the mill at Manor Parsley. According to the Women's Institute scrapbook, *"He placed each farmer's sacks in a special place, he ground the corn and returned it to its place, knowing when each farmer's quota was finished. In order to open the dam he had to cross the stream by a narrow plank over which he walked without faltering."*

The mill was worked by a waterwheel, to the right of the row of buildings which are now largely derelict. The water to drive it came via a leat from the stream across the road, just a little uphill from the mill. It collected in the mill pool and was released to cross under the road as required.

Circa 1900...The Mill at Manor Parsley

Dennis Barbary has lived at Manor Parsley all of his life and his mother, Nora Penhaul, was a niece to Miller Matthews. He said that the area was referred to as Mill Pool but he didn't rule out the possibility that it was called Parsley at that time. He was, however, more certain of the reason for its claim to being a manor. He said, *"I think that my grandfather, Alfred Penhaul, erected the sign Manor Parsley on the mill cottage as a joke and by so doing he started the myth."* This always seemed likely and we have certainly not found anyone with a better suggestion for the derivation of the name.

The remains of another mill are in a field at the foot of Gover Hill; where bones were ground to dust for use as manure.

We are not sure which mill Thomas Nankivell operated in the 1850s; it may well have been one of those already mentioned.

Farmers listed in various trade directories:

William Dadd, *Coosagwartha* (probably *Coosewartha*) ... 1856.
Richard Garland ... 1856 to 1862.
James Harris, Banns ... 1856 to 1862.
John Lowrey, Gover ... 1856 to 1862.
John Rodda, Menagissey ... 1856 to 1897.
Henry Walters, Menagissey ... 1856 to 1897.
John Cock, Banns ... 1862.
James Harris, Gover, *Lower Trenithick* ... 1873 to 1878.
William Kessel ... 1873.
John J Nettle, *Mansion House Farm* ... 1873 to 1897.
William Richards, Gover ... 1873.
Thomas Miller, market gardener, Banns Hill ... 1878 to 1930.
William Harris, *Trevipick Farm (possibly Trevisick)* ... 1878.
James Mark Moyle, *Stencoose* ... 1878 to 1923.
Charles Reed, *Banns Farm* ... 1878.
Martin & Henry Richards, *Trenithick Farm* ... 1878 to 1897.
Samuel Rodda, Menagissey ... 1878 and 1883.
Joseph Thomas, *Coosewartha* ... 1878 to 1883.
Anthony Williams, *Towan Farm* ... 1878.
Henry Willoughby, *Goynes Farm*, Menagissey ... 1878 to 1897.
Solomon Paul James, Banns ... 1883 to 1893.
Edward Rodda, *Lower Trenithick* ... 1883 to 1906.
Nathaniel Snell, *Trevisick* ... 1883 to 1889.
William Tonkin, Splat ... 1883 to 1923.
William Henry Cummins, Menagissey ... 1889 to 1914.
Charles Garland, *Princecroft Farm*, Shortcross ... 1889 to 1919.
George Thomas, *Coosewartha* ... 1889.
John Williams ... 1889 (also a carrier).
Robert Williams, *Banns Vale* ... 1889 to 1893.

Henry Cock, *Banns Vale*...1893 to 1906.

Thomas Kestle...1893 to 1935.

Henry Rodda, Shortcross...1893 to 1939.

Edward Snell, *Trevisick*...1893 to 1914.

Richard Walters, *Prince's Croft*...1893 to 1897.

Mark James, Banns...1897 to 1902.

William Matthews, Mill Pool...1897 to 1910.

Mrs Mary Rogers, *Wingfield House*...1897 to 1902.

Joseph Eslick, *Mansion House Farm*...1902.

Eldred Richards, Menagissey...1902 to 1923.

Mrs Elizabeth Richards, *Trenithick*...1902 to 1923 (over 150 acres).

Richard John Rodda...1902 to 1906 (also a carpenter).

Aldred Tremewan, Menagissey...1902 to 1906.

Richard Jenkin, *Croft Prince*...1906 to 1939.

William Bassett, Banns....1910 to 1930.

William Morley Cock, *Banns Vale*...1910.

Joseph Jose...1910.

William John Matthews...1910 to 1914.

Robert Nicholas, Menagissey...1910 to 1926.

Thomas Robbins, market gardener, *Wheal Allen*
(probably *Wheal Ellen*)...1910.

Richard Rodda...1910 to 1939.

Samuel Rodda, *Lower Trenithick*...1910 to 1930.

Charles Thomas...1910 to 1935.

Mrs Bessie Tremewan, Menagissey...1910 to 1930.

Edwin Brokenshire, *Banns Vale*...1914.

Richard Henry Carter, *Goose Wartha* (probably *Coosewartha*)...
1914 to 1939.

John Jeffery, *Rose Farm*...1914 to 1919.

Mrs Joseph Jose...1914 to 1923.

Mrs William (Bessie) Matthews, Mill Pool...1914 to 1930.

Alfred Ernest Rodda, Menagissey...1914 to 1939.

Edwin Rowe, *Wheal Allan* (probably *Wheal Ellen*)...1914 to 1939.

Percival Commins, Menagissey...1919 to 1923.

Robert Matthews, market gardener, *Banns Vale*...1919.

John Pryor...1919 to 1926.

Samuel Waters...1919 to 1923.

James Garland, *Princecroft Farm*...1923 to 1926.

Mrs Jane Jose, Mount Hawke Halt... 1923 to 1939.
Joseph Julyan, smallholder, *Banns Vale*... 1926 to 1939.
John Algar... 1930.
Hesketh Arthur E Coryn, *Croft Prince*... 1930 to 1935.
George Percy Kestle... 1930 to 1939.
John Henry Parsons, *Wheal Ellen*... 1930 to 1939.
John Charles Roberts, Gover... 1930 (over 150 acres).
William Rogers, Menagissey... 1930.
Gordon Thomas, Menagissey... 1930 to 1935.
Mrs A Tonkin, Splat... 1930.
Richard Pearce Gould... 1935 to 1939.
Alfred Penhaul, Mill Pool... 1935 to 1939.
Mrs Eva Jane Roberts, *Gover Farm*... 1935 to 1939 (over 150 acres).
Victor Roberts, *Lower Trenithick*... 1935.
Mrs Mary Roberts Rogers, Menagissey... 1935.
James Watts, Splat... 1935 to 1939.
John Benjamin, Menagissey... 1939.
James Henry Green, *Lower Trenithick*... 1939.

Poultry farming has a long history in the village, there was one located in Park Shady and another in Rope Walk, operated by Graham and Angela Parsons.

The milk supply for the village came from a number of local farms but according to Mary George there were always plenty of customers and they never considered the other suppliers to be their competitors. Her family sold their produce from 1920 to 1991, either in their shop or direct to the door. Even when they ceased farming in 1959 the milk round continued, up until 1991 when Mary retired.

Mary George delivering the milk which she did up until 1991

Joe Julian from Banns was another early supplier; he travelled the village with his pony and cart serving milk from a churn. It seems that Winnie Green took over his round before passing it on to Alan and Pauline Green. Shirley Barrett recorded that Mrs Green left her bed at four in the morning to cut cabbages, returned home by 7.00am to help Jimmy with the milking and after breakfast she delivered the milk. Tough old life wasn't it?

Phil Thomas farmed at *Lower Banns Farm* from the early 1930s to 1948. He then took over *Banns Vale* from Mr Julian, one of the local milk providers, and farmed there until he died in 1974. Phil was born near Mawla, shortly after his parents had returned home from America. He had three children, Donald (born in 1929, at Banns), Nancy (later Colman) and Wendy (later Beard). From a young age his son Donald worked both at home on the farm and for Neddie Mewton, on the threshing sets. You will read some of his stories later. He married Marcella Greenslade in 1956 and around that time began working for G A Carlyon, initially on a part-time basis. In October 1960 he commenced a 30-year career at South Crofty Mine as a whim driver and then as an instructor.

Charles (Charlie) and Ellen Richards were at *Coosewartha Farm* from the late 1930s to 1956; they moved to there from Mawla. Their grandson, Monty Burrows, recalled that some of their children and their families lived there with them. It was a council-owned farm and when Charles died the remainder of the family were not considered to have sufficient agricultural knowledge to run the farm and they had to move out.

The Garland Family lived at *Henly House* and owned some of the land to the rear. Francis Garland had trained as a pilot in the RAF during the Second World War but illness meant that he had to be invalided out. He decided to become a market gardener, erected two large greenhouses, and was soon supplying a network of shops. Donald Thomas joined him in one venture and they planted an acre of peas; as he said, *"That's an awfully lot of pods to pick."* Francis later ceased growing and concentrated on wholesale and then retail provision.

Monty and Phyllis Rodda farmed in the centre of the village but this has already been mentioned with his activities as the village smithy. Their daughter, Diana, now has a gardening business. She carries out decorating and other odd jobs but with a business name of DIGGIT the emphasis is clearly on horticulture.

Ted and Cicely Skimins moved to Mount Hawke sometime around 1960 and purchased some land near where the new school was later built. Ted recalled walking his cows from his smallholding through the village, a sight that would now seem strange. The cows had to make their way up Back Lane (now Roddas Road); it was then just a narrow pathway with brambles and bushes on each side. They then crossed Shortcross Road and into his fields, where *Milden* now stands. Another route was along the road in front of the Men's Institute, down past the post office and up to his fields in Rope Walk.

It was not until the bungalows were built along its length that Back Lane was cleared of bracken and renamed Roddas Road. According to John Jotcham the name change was not appreciated by everyone, Mrs Cowling, the baker, asked, *"What's going on now then? It's always been Back Lane; bit posh isn't it?"*

In 1981 Ted and Cicely sold most of their smallholding to the owners of the rapidly expanding Cumber Homes project but even in 2008 he still has some connection with produce through the sale of vegetables from his front gate.

John Wilkins (sometimes referred to as John Wilkin) was married to Elizabeth (Bessie) Dabb. He was a prop man at Wheal Coates and spent some time working in the gold mines in India. He was also a farmer, at *Menagissey Farm*, and is listed in trade directories from 1914 to 1930. Bessie appears as the farmer in the 1935 and 1939 directories and members of the family are still there. One of John's sons has already been mentioned, Harold Wilkins, a local blacksmith, born at *Arbor Cottage* in 1902. Harold later moved to 4 Alexandra Terrace where son Peter was born.

Jack Rowe was a market gardener at Menagissey during the 1950s and employed quite a number of local people. He lived at *Oceana* (now *The Perch*) and his land stretched down into the valley towards Navvy Pit.

Manor Parsley Farm is located at the bottom of the hill from Menagissey; the farmhouse is on the left and the fields on the right. Jack Barbary took over the farm in the mid 1930s from Mr Waters. At that time it was only about 12 acres but additional land was gradually purchased increasing it to about 100 acres. From 1985 to 1995 Dennis Barbary farmed it before passing it to his nephew, Paul Bache, who is still there.

In her collection of notes and stories about the village Shirley Barrett refers to the waterwheel near the wooden bridge across the stream in Park Shady. This provided water to *Trevissick Farm* (sometimes *Trevisick Farm*) until the end of the Second World War. A visit here at the appropriate time of year would explain why it was called Bluebell Woods. A story tells of a trapdoor in one of the cottages; it is said to have an underground chamber with tunnels leading to the sea. *Trevissick* seems to have had a ghost who was endlessly searching for something until one night a storm demolished a section of wall and exposed a hoard of gold coins...allegedly.

Edwin (Neddie) Mewton (1901-1963) worked for G A Carlyon from around 1920 and often had to drive a steam engine up-country to collect equipment for the mines. His son-in-law, David Hall, recalled some of Neddie's stories. *"A trip to Devon was a major run in a steam engine and he could be away for days. On one occasion, when he was bringing back a Lancashire Boiler, he was going down Tuckingmill hill with another engine at the rear, to hold the load back. Neddie stopped to change gear but the other driver didn't and a shove from behind pushed the lead engine into the tram tracks. He went all the way to the bottom of the hill before he could get out.*

On another occasion Neddie and Gordon Snell were on a long trip and decided to spend the night in a barn. They found an old tarpaulin hanging up and decided to sleep in it. They brought the 'Devil' (fire brazier) in from the engine and placed it under their 'hammock.' Unfortunately the tarpaulin had been coated with tar and as it warmed their bed became increasing moist...with alarming results."

Neddie turned to running a butcher's shop and after a few years, in the early 1940s, he also started an agricultural contracting business although in those days it probably didn't operate with such a grand name. This was the era of the threshing machine, operated with steam engines; later he also used a David Brown tractor. One of his engines was a seven-horse power Fowler, registration AF 3581, which he called *Millennium King* after one of the engines he drove for G A Carlyon.

Neddie's elder daughter, Lorna, recalled having to do her bit in the business either on the threshing set scraping the dowse away or by tending the stationary binder which, she said, used wire to bind the bales rather than twine. She said, *"He was mad on steam engines, he even named me after one that he drove for Carlyon's."*

Donald Thomas worked part-time for Neddie, driving the steam engine. He recalled one job on a farm near the Truro Crematorium, *"I had to drive through Truro main-street towing the threshing set, the bailer and a dilly which was a trailer carrying the wood. It was fair length and the steel wheels on the cobbles made quite a noise; I was only 15 at the time."*

Neddie Mewton at the wheel of his David Brown tractor

The David Brown tractor towing the threshing set down Gover Hill

Claude Tonkin recalled a number of local chaps who worked for Neddie including Leslie Faithful Blitchford, known as *Major* or *Bullet Head*. A distinguishing feature was his Welly boots, worn on most occasions. Norman Dell was another; he had worked in a corn mill in his younger days and was described to us as a test pilot for Teagles. Apparently he rode a motorised bicycle and was such a good advertisement for it that the company didn't charge him for any replacements. His trademark features were his peak cap, stick and brown suit. His health was not good in later life but he was a familiar character around the village…in the Men's Institute or in Bill Jolly's workshop for *a bit chat.*

Photographer Ken Young was there with his camera to capture this working scene…
Donald Thomas piling up straw

A quick break for a photo call on threshing day at Four Gates, near the cricket field, for Phil Thomas of
Bann's Vale Farm…the rally engine Millennium King is in use
(L to R) Jack Wilkins, Gilbert Roberts (Gover Farm), Joe Penhall, Phil Thomas, (Donald Thomas'
father), Donald Wilkins (Jack's son), Steve unknown, Neddie Mewton, George Hines (Towan Cross)
and unknown boy (Photo by Ken Young)

Neddie later purchased a rally engine, a single cylinder compound Burrell. It was called *Ponto* but he renamed it *Millennium King,* once again taking the name from a G A Carlyon engine.

This was truly a boy's toy, his pride and joy, and he delighted in showing it at the rallies and carnivals around Cornwall. Donald Thomas, Claude Tonkin and David Hall were often enlisted to help.

David said, *"Sometime in the 1950s we were on our way back from St Evel Rally and couldn't believe our bad luck. Reggie Morse was driving and I was in the wagon waving the cars past. A nice looking cream Ford Anglia came up behind us and I waved him on. He pulled out but unfortunately so did Reggie and one of the engine hubcaps scraped the side of the car. The Anglia driver stopped just ahead of us and waved us down. He asked who owned the vehicle and Neddie said that it was his. We looked at the car and there was a scar right down the side, the metal work was sound but the entire thickness of paint had been planed off. The bit about the bad luck; he was a Police Sergeant, it was a brand new car and it cost Neddie £35 for repairs."*

A few years later Neddie took part in Chacewater Carnival and managed to beat the famous *Gladiator* into second place. This was quite an achievement and he was delighted to be invited to lead the Carnival. After it was over he went to collect his prize money…from Arnold Hodge's house. Donald Thomas said, *"After a while Neddie re-appeared, a little worse for wear; he'd clearly decided to celebrate the win."* David said, *"He was certainly pleased with himself and he came out as p***** as a mattress but you can't print that."*

They hauled him onboard and sat him on the toolbox but he didn't look too safe so they put him in the coalbunker and covered him up with a sack. The trouble was that every time they wanted some coal they had to prop him up so that they could shovel it from under him. David said, *"Next day all he could talk about was his sore backside, or words to that effect."*

Neddie Mewton on one of his traction engines

Chris Williams ran the St Agnes Coach Company, he was keen on steam engines and always pleased to be involved. Donald recalled a rally at St Erth when they had to tow a four-wheeled trailer, the platform for compere Jack Trounson. He said, *"There were three of us on the engine, Claude, Chris and myself and we always called that a proper old nuisance as we were in each other's way. When we stopped in Redruth for water I noticed that there was only one person on one of the other engines so I said, 'Cookie, do you want a steersman?' With that Chris swapped engines and we were passing each other all the way down."*

Donald Thomas described Claude Tonkin as a superb driver. He said, *"He really took a pride in driving a straight line. A lot of people couldn't do that, they would weave all over the place but not Claude. You could look back and see the line where the wheels had been, it was as straight as a die."*

Millennium King steaming up through the village

Farming is no longer a daily feature of village life and we rarely see a long procession of cows dropping their *gifts* on our pristine roads. The majestic shires are reserved for special occasions and the evocative sound of the clanging metal churns is gone forever, except perhaps, in our heads... a memory that does not fade.

Mining

Mining activity in the area was extensive and the village of Mount Hawke was founded on that industry. Its raison d'etre was to provide homes for the tin and copper miners and the village grew in response to that need.

The mining industry has a fascinating history, well documented and recorded by those with a greater knowledge of it than us. A book about a mining village could not ignore that industry however but we have restricted our coverage to the social and political aspects, the written and spoken stories and information *borrowed* from other sources.

In his book *The Metalliferous Mining Region of South-West England,* H G Dines talks of a copper belt surrounding the tin centre and of the copper mines between St Agnes and Porthtowan being at their prime about the middle of the nineteenth century.

A section in John Kinsman's book, *The Cornish Handbook,* says, *"Beyond Truro, the visitor finds himself in the mining district, among men and boys who go to mysterious work in suits stained with mundic, wearing candles in their hats; whose talk is of things hidden fathoms underground. The Cornish are a secretive race, and have an instinct for searching by skill and faith in dark places, whether with nets dropped down through the floor of the sea, or with cages and buckets lowered into the bowels of the earth."*

He refers to a dirge over the mining industry by W Copeland Borlase, President of the Royal Institution of Cornwall in May 1879, who said, *"Scan the landscape far and near; in the features of it there is little variety; the hollow crumbling tower, the roofless account-houses, the piles of 'attel' smothering the soil, the ring-fence enclosing the abandoned shaft… these same objects repeat themselves whichever way you turn, the tale of an industry which for the present at least, if not for ever, has departed from amongst us, carrying with it not only the loss of surplus wealth to one class (which is a small matter), but well nigh of life itself."*

In 1920 John talked of the tin and copper mining industry being under a cloud but spoke of those who confidently looked for an early revival, *"… believing that the area around Carn Brea is still the richest mineral deposit in all the world."* He talked of mining in the St Agnes Parish and of it involving some of the best miners in the world who, he said, *"When their task was finished, they climbed ladders clamped to the perpendicular side of the shaft for hundreds of feet. There was only one way in which that weary climb after a hard day's work could be avoided; and that was so dangerous as to be almost suicidal. The rock,* blasted by means of gunpowder and dynamite, was taken to the surface in huge buckets, or kibbles, drawn up by a wire rope which received its power from the engine at the top of the shaft. As the kibbles were drawn up, they rocked ominously from side to side; and occasionally some reckless man would jump from the level, or passage, leading into the shaft, in order that he might catch the rope of the quickly ascending bucket and so ride to the surface, instead of climbing the wearisome succession of ladders. To miss the object would mean certain death, for, even if one escaped the jagged rocks which lined the shaft, the fall would destroy consciousness and at the bottom there would be water of almost unknown depth."

An article in the St Agnes Museum Trust Journal by Betty Tredinnick about life in the St Agnes Parish up to about 1840 said, "Again from Peterville to Trevaunance all along the field at the foot of Town Hill there were stamps and tin floors. Similarly the valleys at Mingoose, Chapel Porth and Banns in Mount Hawke were all full of water wheels and stamps, employing many men and women."

Long before its popularity as a place of pleasure the beach at Porthtowan provided employment for those men who worked to extract minerals from its sands or from the residue of the mining activity further up stream...the tin streamers. These men could be found in most mining locations long after deep mining was discontinued.

Most of the mines in the area had closed by the third quarter of the 19th century; the exception seems to be Tywarnhayle, which lingered on with intermittent success.

Circa 1904...Tin streaming on Porthtowan Beach

Trenithic Mine was described by Dines as an old mine located to the north of Mount Hawke, between Gover and the old corn mill. It is identified on the 1907 OS Map as, *"Tin, disused."*

Prince Royal Mine was a copper and tin mine and seems to have been located in Banns valley, it may well have been a part of the Trenithick Mine. On the 8th April 1825 the *West Briton* reported that a most valuable discovery of copper had been made in the Prince Royal Mine and that the workings of that mine underlie the village of Mount Hawke.

Great St Vincent was developed to extract copper and lead ore and was situated on the eastern outskirts of Mount Hawke village, probably out near where the Skatepark is now located. It operated in the early 1800s and had two adits, one of which, Gover Adit, commenced near the millpond and was once used for the St Agnes water supply.

The old millpond at Gover

North Hallenbeagle was a copper mine situated to the northeast of Mount Hawke, to the east of Great St Vincent and out towards the Truro/St Agnes road.

East Wheal Music may well have been an independent operation but information is sparse. Its name is linked with both North Hallenbeagle and Great St Vincent.

Wheal Music (Navvy Pit) produced mainly copper and was situated about a mile up the valley from the Porth, on the north side of the Porthtowan to Mount Hawke road. It became a surface-worked mine with an excavated area of about an acre and to a depth of approximately 150 feet.

Ashley Rowe referred to Mount Hawke and its copper mine and tells the story of the huge pit adjacent to the road from the village to Porthtowan. Wheal Music is a name on the map but it acquired the dreary name of Navvy Pit. *"Where the road from Truro joins that from Redruth, immediately before entering the desolate canyon-like valley that leads to Porthtowan, there is a huge circular pit; all that remains of a once notable mine. A post office letter-box placed on a nearby bridge shows the name Navvy Pit."*

There are many references in early newspapers to Wheal Music. An advertisement in the *Royal Cornwall Gazette* of the 14th February 1807 contained details of a sale by auction of, *"16,123 shares in Wheal Music Mine, St Agnes, which mine is now working by a water engine and wherein is an exceedingly rich course of ore, lately discovered at the depth of only six fathoms under the surface."*

Six fathoms is only 36 feet; the actual ore was nearly at surface level. The term *exceedingly rich* was justified, the intersection of two lodes resulted in bunches of almost pure copper.

On the 10th June 1820 the *West Briton* reported a fatality, William Tambly was killed in one of the levels by a fall of earth.

Circa 1900 … A view of Gardiner's Shaft at Tywarnhayle Mine with Navvy Pit (Wheal Music) in the foreground

The mining historian Hamilton Jenkin refers to Captain Oates of Rose-in-Vale, Mithian, who, in the 1830s, reputedly profited by £30,000 from Wheal Music. The Revd W Haslam preached a revival meeting on the lawn of Rose-in-Vale and in his book, *From Death into Life* refers to Captain Oates as the chief parishioner, an uneducated man who had risen from the rank of a common miner to that of a mine captain. He further describes him as being very shrewd and clever and as having succeeded in accumulating a considerable sum of money. He goes on to say, *"Being the wealthy man of the parish, he sat on Sunday in the large square pew; but beyond giving personal attendance, and that very regularly, I do not know what other heed he gave, either to the service or the sermon."* In another book, Capt Oates is described as one of the mining kings of the day and Captain William Roberts in his book *Perranporth* describes him as uneducated, thrifty, genial and considerate with all. Captain Oates died with no direct relatives and was buried at Perranzabuloe Parish Church.

It seems that the mine closed for a while and when it re-opened, in 1852, many of the old workings had collapsed. Open working was later adopted but this method was not viewed well by the workers especially when they were referred to as navvies rather than miners; it was then that the name of Wheal Music became eclipsed by the rather derogatory name of Navvy Pit. During the 1980s the pit was gradually filled and the area levelled.

Navvy Pit being filled in the 1980s

East Wheal Ellen was a small copper mine situated at Menagissey and according to Frank Carpenter in *A Millennium Chronicle*, a Mr Greenwood and others started it in 1856 with 1,300 shares.

Captain William Boundy of Mount Hawke is listed in the Cornwall Trade Directory of 1850s and 1860s as a mine agent and steward to Humphrey Willyams esquire of Truro. He lived at Banns, in the house now called *Trenarth*.

There are a few houses of comparative grandeur in the village; the homes of people who held important positions in the community. They are mostly in the older areas of the village, at Menagissey and in Banns Valley and *Trenarth* is one such house. It was built in the 1830s and is now owned by Effie and John Harvie.

Mining Agent, Captain Robert Williams purchased the property in the late 1800s and lived there with his wife, Mary, and family. It is probable that it was he who greatly enlarged the house and named it *Trenarth*. Their daughter, also Mary, married Joseph Langdon who left the area to work in Australia. In 1891 Mary aged 38 was living there with their infant daughter, Mildred; Joseph was presumably still in Australia. Mildred Langdon lived there for many years and in the early 1930s she built two bungalows on the opposite side of the road for her staff...Claude Tonkin's father was her gardener/chauffeur. During the 1980s Colonel Basil Wilson and his wife, Marcia, purchased the property; she was the mother of actor Oliver Reed.

We are indebted to Mr and Mrs Harvie for much of this information; they have lived at *Trenarth* since 1987.

A number of mines line the valley that sweeps down to Porthtowan; Wheal Ellen, South Ellen and Tywarnhayle (Wheal Rock), the scene of one of the worst above ground mining accidents in Cornwall. These and the many that line the coast will be included in our later book covering Mawla, Porthtowan and Towan Cross.

The work of the miners was hard and often dangerous, the workings often went to a great depth with the consequent risk of rock falls. In the main it was not well paid but on occasions the rewards were good as this story from the Women's Institute scrapbook suggests. *"Some of the miners were paid on a kind of piece work basis known as tribute. Miss Rodda's grandfather must have had a lucky strike one day. When he arrived home to his wife he drew out of his pocket a £5 note and asked, 'Is that enough?' She, being a wise woman replied, 'Not if there is more!' So he pulled out another, 'Is that enough?' Again the answer came, 'Not if there is more!' Question and answer continued until at least £20 was on the table. When one considers the value compared with our present value one realises the force of the story."*

The valleys at each end of the village, at Gover and Manor Parsley, are said to be joined by a tunnel or adit, a subterranean stroll would pass under Trenithick Estate and the graveyard. Olga Grant claimed that her blind uncle, George Tallack, once completed the walk, or maybe the crawl. We cannot confirm the accuracy of this nor are we going to check it out.

Writing about Tywarnhale Mine in the St Agnes Museum Trust Journal, Robin Smith wrote the following; it serves well as an end to this chapter. *"It seems strange to think of this now quiet, peaceful valley once echoing to industrial noise and providing income for as many as 400 workers. During the economic life of the mine, social and working conditions were relatively harsh and mining was a risky operation but, unfortunately, apart from limited agricultural work, employment was scarce. However, the Cornish miner and his family adjusted to the hazardous life underground and reports of accidents or fatalities were simply absorbed with as little fuss as possible."*

Roads & Railway

The Railway

Most advances in community life are incremental but every so often there is a step-change that touches everyone's life. The coming of the railway must have been one of those occasions.

On the 6th July 1903 the line from Chacewater to Perranporth came into use and the sight of smoke rising from the cuttings was witnessed for the first time. Just 100 years after Trevithick had run his steam locomotive at Penydarren, the railway had arrived in this corner of Cornwall. People could now travel to any place in the country linked by steel rails providing, of course, they could afford the fare. Completion of the line from Perranporth to Newquay took a little longer; it opened on the 2nd January 1905.

Mount Hawke Halt was commissioned on the 16th August 1905 and described in Kelly's Trade Directory as, *"A halting place on the Perranporth and Newquay electric branch of the Great Western Railway."* Despite it being a *brave way* from the village it was of great benefit to the community.

In the first Journal of the St Agnes Museum Trust John Redfearn described it thus. *"The branch line started at Blackwater East on a fairly sharp curve of one furlong, two chains radius, which, incidentally, apart from a similar one at Perranporth, was the most severe on the whole route. It then continued in a northerly direction from Blackwater Junction North up a steep gradient of I in 60 for six furlongs, under the road at Hellenbeagle Bridge where a road diversion was necessary, then falling 1 in 60 it came to Mount Hawke Halt, 1½ miles from Chacewater Station.*

Mount Hawke Halt was situated just below the bridge on the Chiverton to Mount Hawke road and was in keeping with many of the stations and halts on the branch line in that they were some distance from the villages from which they took their name, somewhat surprising in view of the purpose of the halt, a GWR invention, which was to bring the railway as close as possible to small communities.

From Mount Hawke the railway continued on its north all the time rising, first at 1 in 60, a curve to the left then right, past Gover Farm, under the road at Sandy Lane crossroads and out on to the embankment on the approach to St Agnes Station, where the gradient was a rising of 1 in 182. Almost ahead, on the left, the passenger would have a grand view of the Beacon dominating the sea and countryside all around at 640 feet above sea level and the village of St Agnes lying below it to the north east."

Circa 1900 ... Mount Hawke Railway Halt being excavated by Irish navvies ...
no health & safety rules in those days

The halt as it was when opened in 1905 with its wooden platform and no shelter

In 1905 the St Agnes correspondent for the Royal Cornwall Gazette wrote in despair at the management of the train service on the Newquay to Chacewater line. He observed that passengers had to cool their heels while their temperatures rose as they waited for a connection at Chacewater Station. It was a cold spot in winter and he told of their mortification at seeing an empty motor train pass through while they waited for theirs. (RCG 30/11/05)

The halt during its working life … by now the wooden platform has been replaced with concrete and the traditional pagoda shelter is in place

Like so many people from Mount Hawke, and beyond, Peter Wilkins caught the train at the halt, he said, *"I was often walking along the road when I saw a column of smoke rising as the train approached the halt, I then had to run. Mr Dawe was one of the guards, he was a big man; his daughter was head teacher at Mount Hawke School."* Of course, the area served by the halt extended far beyond the village and for some there was a choice of departure points. Folk in Blackwater had to decide between Mount Hawke Halt and Chacewater Station while in Silverwell it was Mount Hawke, Mithian or Goonbell … happy days.

But all things come to an end and sad to say that applied to the local network. The history of our railway line is quite short … just sixty years. In that time it served the local populace and delivered many holidaymakers to their destination; it was an age when such a journey was considered to be a part of the holiday. It employed local people and underwent the change from steam to diesel. But in 1963 it closed. With indecent haste its track was removed, halts destroyed and its cuttings backfilled. In *Blackwater and its Neighbours* we wrote that it was felled by the Beeching axe but it seems we were wrong, it closed just before he began his savage cuts. There are still many features to remind us of its route, the bridges, viaducts and the scars across the countryside but now we are left with little more than our memories and perhaps some anger at a lost opportunity.

The halt immediately following closure in 1963…
the name board and oil lamps have already been removed

By the 1970s the tracks have been removed and nature has started to reclaim the land. Since this picture the cutting has been filled and is now an access road to the West of England Steam Rally site

Road Transport

Whether or not we credit the wheel with being the greatest invention of all time it is indisputable that it has been of tremendous benefit to mankind. It was no accident that carpenters and blacksmiths located their workshops next to each other as they joined forces to produce the wheels necessary for the early vehicles. Wagons and carts snaked across the countryside with scant regard to logic; lanes and pathways were established almost by chance, routes which had been trudged for centuries. They meandered this way and that perhaps to avoid natural hazards or maybe just to accommodate the whim of the horse and the wild animals that once roamed this land.

Little changed over the generations and it was not until the introduction of the *horseless carriage* that roads began to be straightened and consideration given to any sort of surfacing.

Local committees were set up during the 1800s and each of these Boards of Highways was given jurisdiction over the roads within its boundaries. Surveyors were appointed with the power to undertake necessary improvements and to employ local people to break stone for repairs. Many rural main roads were not surfaced with tarmac until the 1930s and even then it was not welcomed by all with many protests from wagoners whose horses could not maintain sufficient grip on the smooth surface as they hauled their heavy loads to the nearby ports.

Long before any form of transport was widely available, people walked … to their workplace, to the shops and for pleasure. Shank's pony was the chief means of transport for most people who thought nothing of a five-mile hike into Redruth and back.

Horseback or pony and cart were an option for those who could afford it. Tom was a village character in his own right, a horse owned by the Blackney family of Mount Hawke. On one occasion when he broke loose Mrs Pearce's mother tried to stop him, she stood in a narrow lane with her arms outstretched. Tom wasn't having it, he took a flying leap clean over her and continued his wanderings. (W I book 1950)

During the latter part of the 19th century cheap transport arrived in the form of the horse bus; it travelled to Truro on Wednesdays and Redruth on Fridays … market days. It was popular and often there were many people crammed on board. A heavy load for the horses especially on hills when the passengers were expected to dismount and walk, perhaps even to push. Shirley Barrett recorded that passengers boarded the bus at the church and travelled out to where the railway halt was later built; it then turned right, towards Blackwater. The bus was pulled by two horses and had a large tarpaulin to be pulled up to provide cover in the event of rain.

In his series of books entitled *Travelling to Truro*, Roger Grimley tells of John Libby who by 1873 was running a van to and from Truro on Mondays, Wednesdays and Saturdays; and to Redruth on Fridays. The Cornwall Trade Directory records that he was running even earlier, in 1856, *"Libby, from Mounthawke (to Truro), Wednesday & Saturday, returning same days."*

The horse-drawn service was then taken over by local farmer John L Williams who is listed as a carrier in 1878 and 1889 where it states, *"Carrier to Truro, Wednesday and Saturday; Redruth, Friday."* He was the grandfather of Mary and Donald George who are mentioned in other sections of this book. He later moved with his family to Cubert. In 1920 his daughter, Edith, and her husband, Wesley, moved to Mount Hawke to take over a shop and *Wingfield Farm*.

In the 1890s, the bus service passed to yet another farmer, John Nicholls. William John Matthews of Manor Parsley took over sometime around 1900 and is included in the Kelly's Directory up to 1906. From information provided by Will Jones, the cobbler's son, we know that he had a bus house on the left of the hill down to Banns, almost opposite the old cobbler's shop. Mr Grimley says that he had been the driver on the service since at least 1880.

Circa 1905...The single storey bus house (centre picture)

The Women's Institute scrapbook states that sometime between the two world wars the Western National Omnibus Company (formerly the CMT or Cornish Motor Transport Company) established a route from Redruth to Perranporth via Mount Hawke travelling up Church Hill and on to St Agnes. After some years the route was changed to include Porthtowan.

Joan Chynoweth was told that the CMT service started the week that she was born, in 1922. Prior to that the villagers only had a service to Redruth on Fridays. Clearly, the people of Mount Hawke didn't go out of the village much. In 1927 it became a National Omnibus & Transport route and later the Western National Service.

Harold Pearce is listed as a carrier in the 1930, 1935 and 1939 trade directories but this may have been for goods only.

Peter Wilkins recalled that during the 1950s his mother had a use for the bus service, it was typical of the age. He said, *"My father was the blacksmith at Wheal Rose and my mother would send him a pasty on the bus. She would wrap it up and conductress Rose Trenerry would stop the bus and take it in to him. I don't think they'd do that these days."*

At that time there was no service to Truro indeed, it was not until after the Second World War, in 1946, that Malcolm Carter of Mount Hawke began a daily service from Porthtowan, through Mount Hawke and Blackwater, to Truro.

Margaret Carter recalled that he purchased a plot of land from Wesley George, in Rope Walk, on the right just below where the council houses were built. *"Malcolm built a bus garage there and installed his own petrol tanks and pump. It's all been demolished now and replaced by houses."*

Malcolm's brother, Edgar, returned to Cornwall to join him in the early 1950s and the business name changed to Carter Brothers' Coaches.

Roger Grimley describes the Carter's fleet as a 1937 ... 20 seat Bedford WTB, a 1946 ... 32 seat Commer Commando, a 1948 ... 32 seat Commer Commando, a 1949 ... 29 seat Commer Q4, a 1947 ... 26 seat Bedford OB, a 1949 ... 31 seat Commer Avenger 1 and a 1952 ... 35 seat Commer Avenger 1.

That's as technical as we get but for those interested in the history of motor transport in Cornwall then Roger's books will prove to be a fascinating read. These can be obtained from Old Post, Bigbury, Kingsbridge, Devon, TQ7 4AP.

During the Suez Crisis special runs were arranged to take workers to Falmouth Docks, probably an attempt to cut down on the use of private cars to conserve fuel supplies.

Lack of support was the reason for discontinuing the workers and shoppers service to Porthtowan in 1962; it had run for 16 years.

Malcolm Carter with one of the fleet

In 1964 Malcolm Carter sold his coach business and took over the Chiverton Cross garage.

The new owner was Brian Hopley who continued to garage the vehicles at Rope Walk. When Brian died in 1999 his son, Nick, took over. He said, *"When I joined in 1988 we had four vehicles and as the number began to grow we needed larger premises. In 2005 we re-located to Gover Farm where we had the space to develop the business. We did this with tours, school runs and an increase in the number of service runs, we now have 17 vehicles."*

Road layouts change and we quickly forget the old route, names alter too and are so often lost to time. While the standard of road maintenance may not always be what is expected, we do not have to go back more than two or three generations to find dirt tracks in place of bitmac.

The original Penhaul Lane ran through what is now Trenithick Estate, it is now Penhallow Way. But the old name lives on even if the spelling has changed; Penhall Lane is the narrow road which leads from the old cobbler's shop down to the Trenithick Corn Mill. A hand-written note on a copy of the 1907 OS Map refers to this as Plummer's Road, no doubt after the miller who plied his trade a little further down the hill. It has also been referred to as The Butts. Old Church Lane spurs off from this hill, to where the Penhaul family lived and worked the land and where the old congregational chapel once stood.

Blind Tippett's is a name still remembered; it seems to have been taken from a man who, as the name implies, had lost his sight and who often walked this road. It runs along the eastern boundary of Trenithick Estate (often referred to as Cumber Homes from the name of the development company) from the junction at the top of Gover Hill to the crossroads on the main road into the village from Truro. According to Chris Chynoweth this crossroads was known as *Polly's* or *Polly's Corner;* the road to the railway halt was always referred to as *Going out downs.*

According to Joan Chynoweth, Highfield Road was once known as *Uncle Bill's Road.* It seems that he was an old village character who had nowhere to live until the kindly people of Mount Hawke bought him a caravan. No one knows where it was sited; perhaps it was along this road.

The reports from the Board of Highway make interesting reading and show how decisions were firmly in the hands of local people, uncluttered by bureaucracy and red tape.

A bus makes its way along Shortcross road

Circa 1910 ... A little further along the front street

Cica 1905 ... A group pose for the photographer in Shortcross Road

A view down through the street with Henly House on the left and the chapel in the background...
possibly during the 1930s

These few gems from the minute book of the Waywardens of St Agnes relate to Mount Hawke.

Meeting 1st April 1841:

"Mr Wm Harper applied that the hedge near the bridge at Skinners Bottom be built up. Resolved that the same be built without delay.

Mr Thomas Barkla applied to have a road made from Short Cross to Water's Mill and from Water's Mill to Mawla Lane end. Resolved that Messrs Francis Harris, Arthur Williams, John Nettle, John Letcher and Joseph Newton examine and report at a subsequent Board Meeting."

It seems that it was eventually agreed that the road be continued from Manor Parsley to Short Cross. Seventeen years later, in 1859, it was resolved to build a bridge over the mill leat at Manor Parsley. In November of that year it was agreed, *"that the stones now laying at Manor Parsley connected with the Bridge across the Mill leat be given to any parties which may place the said Bridge thereon."*

The wage paid to road workers was not generous; in 1841 it was 1/9 per day (about 9p) unless the surveyor could find men who would work for less. Women were also employed but instructions were given that no family or single worker was to earn more than 10/- per week (50p).

An item from April 1843 states *"Mr Richard Harvey having proposed to* build an arch at Gover and fill up the vale and make the road from Peter's House, it was resolved the following persons be appointed to inspect the same and report to the next meeting…"

Capt Gripe was asked to, "Ascertain the height from the river at Gover to Peter Harvey's house and the probable expense of making the proposed road through Mr Harvey's field."

In July it was resolved, "That a new bridge be built at Gover and that a new road be made to pass thro' Mr Harvey's Wellclose field as proposed under the direction and superintendence of the following committee…"

Particulars of the tenders for the work are given in Maurice Bizley's book *Friendly Retreat*. They are quite detailed and are not repeated here. We can say that the work was completed but that is not the end of the story as on the 21st January 1863 the Chairman was requested to admonish Capt Thomas' driver regarding the injury to the road at Gover and ask him to be more careful in future.

The minutes also state that on the 9th February 1854, Henry Waters at Manor Parsley had encroached on the Highways by erecting a threshing machine. It was to be removed or the road be made straight from the corner of New Stickle to the gate at the eastern end of the field where it was to be put back by at least 18 inches.

A letter to the Highway's Board on the 27th November 1890:

> Dear Sir,
>
> I beg to acknowledge receipt of your letter of yesterday's date calling my attention to some damage having been done to the road in the above district and alleged to be done by my traction engine; but you do not say what the damage is. I am not aware of any damage having been done to the roads by my engine but I do remember at the time of my passing over them that they were far from being kept in proper condition.
>
> I would call your attention to the fact that my traction engine is not the only one that has passed over these roads recently and if there is any damage done it may be by the owners or some other cause and not me.
>
> Your obedient Servant
>
> G H Carlyon

A letter dated the 31st October 1899 to the Highway's Board:

Gentlemen,

We beg to call your attention to the desirability of having some pipes placed and paving done on the west side of the road through Mount Hawke village from a point a little below the chapel to the conduit a little above the old post office. In crossing the water table in the parish road leading to what is called the yard, great inconvenience is caused by the sudden jerk of carriages and latterly two upsets having taken place one which led to a rather serious accident to a person named Mr Jones who was confined to his room for some time as a result. We consider the expense to be small in an effectual remedy and trust it will have your attention.

Yours respectfully,

S P James Charles Garland, Wm Tallack, Thos Kestle, William Richards, John Rodda, & Mr Spry.

Circa 1904...Looking down towards Banns. Maude Jones, the cobbler's wife, collects water from the standpipe.

Circa 1910... A cart makes its way towards Banns

We now have a network of roads that our ancestors could only dream of but at considerable cost to the environment and human life. Pollution is an increasing problem and the motor vehicle is charged with being a major contributor. It is also the cause of a tragic waste of human life and perhaps that is not surprising as we hurtle along at high speed, in opposite directions and within a couple of feet of each other. Sadly there is no force for change and we are left to despair that accidents occur with increasing regularity. But while it is unlikely that we will witness the demise of the motor car it seems inevitable that cost and availability will force us into developing some new and energy efficient form of propulsion; surely that will be good for all.

The Chapel

According to Local historian Ashley Rowe, there is no certainty when the name Mount Hawke was first used but we do know that when the Methodist Chapel was built in 1820 the site was described as, *"a piece of land five yards in extent purchased for the erection of a meeting house in Banns, at a place called Mount Hawke."* It seems however that the name did not come into general use at once. (The unit of measurement referred to are a Cornish unit, larger than English yards.)

The chapel taken in 1900 as it was originally built

The original chapel in old Church Lane, between Gover and what is now the Old School public house, was built in the late 1780s; it had been the home of an Independent or Congregational body but was abandoned after the new Methodist Chapel was built. It stood empty for some years and was then taken over by the Anglicans until their new church was completed in 1878.

The Mount Hawke Wesleyan Church centenary booklet produced in 1920 listed the original Trustees as William Tyack, William Martin, William Goyne, Simon Wilkins, James James, Christopher Whitford, James Tonkin, Simon Reynolds, George Martin, John Richards, James Rosewall, Edward Nettall and Francis Harris. Three occupations were represented; a blacksmith, a yeoman and the rest were miners, a reflection of occupational balance of the time. The booklet states, *"It is noteworthy that, despite the restricted educational facilities of that day, each, with one exception, was able to inscribe his name on the trust deeds in a good, legible style…"*

In 1831 four names were added, those of James Nicholas, Richard Richards, John Libby and William Harper.

The author of the booklet is not identified but he, or she, goes on to say, *"It may come as a shock to learn that all the arrangements preliminary to the erection of the chapel were made in a public house."* This was at a Court held at John Opie's in Churchtown, St Agnes. *"A piece of land was purchased for £2 and the transfer was completed by the delivery of a Rod. The Trustees furthermore agreed to pay as rent the sum of two pence per annum. This annual charge was commuted by a cash payment in 1903.*

In 1864 a portion of the field adjoining the chapel was purchased for the sum of five shillings. This allowed the construction of a passage at the south end of the chapel, and provided a means of entering the premises from the rear." Our anonymous writer also tells us that the chapel was registered for marriages on the 6th March 1882.

There is a famous song of the pub with no beer but for many years Mount Hawke was the village with no pub. To explain why, we turn again to the 1920 centenary booklet where it says, *"The cause of Temperance has always found a number of staunch supporters in Mount Hawke and it is probably owing to their implacable antipathy to the drink traffic that the village today rejoices in the fact that it is without a public house."*

But it was not all one way and when a prominent temperance lecturer was asked to speak in the chapel it seemed as though it would split the village. An announcement of the meeting was made from the pulpit in the usual way and when the Minister heard of it he confronted the person who had arranged the meeting.

The Minister said, *"I understand that you have announced a Temperance address for next week in the chapel."*

"I have," replied the Brother.

"It must not take place. I forbid the use of the chapel for such a purpose. I shall lock the door."

The Brother was not to be dissuaded and replied, *"The meeting will take place and if you lock the door I shall burst it open."*

The meeting was held and proved to be the first of many.

They were held in the chapel Methodist schoolroom but were non-denominational and included lantern lectures, services, concerts and dialogues. (W I book 1950)

Historian Ashley Rowe referred to the Teetotal Village in one of his articles for the West Briton when he said that the movement came to Mount Hawke in the 1850s. Miners returning from America, the old forty-niners, had joined the Rechabites and wished to have a lodge in their home village. At that time the Wesleyans were undecided in their attitude towards the movement and matters came to a head when the chapel authorities refused to admit the banners and insignia of the Rechabites. This opposition strengthened the resolve of the teetotal movement and it became all the stronger. Ashley Rowe wrote, *"The public-house, the Red Lion Inn, closed its doors (it was in existence in 1853) and although some beer-shops or kiddley-winks held out for a while, they too had to disappear."*

There is an amusing, though cryptic, account of the last stand in the West Briton of the 6th November 1863. *"The last representative of John Barleycorn also practised the cobbling art but by some means or other, mine host found that leathering the sole and running the spirit was an unprofitable calling. From the best authorities upon the matter we learn that the evil eye of blue ruin was upon the house and the unlucky cobbler escaped from the malevolence of the monster by striking his colours in the night and hoisting 'Mr... shoemaker' the next morning. Since the occurrence of that interesting circumstance, no one has had the temerity to beard the 'Bogie' and things still remain in status quo."*

Referring to the Band of Hope Ashley Rowe reflected that in 1958 there was still no public house in the village and that the banners of the teetotallers were safely housed in the chapel, to be brought forth on successive Band of Hope procession days. He added, *"Not, however, in all the glory of ninety years ago; on Whit-Monday 1861, we learn that this day was kept as a holiday by most people in St Agnes; this was before the passing of Sir John Lubbock's (Holiday) Act. The Mount Hawke Band of Hope, numbering some hundreds of persons, marched in procession from that village to the Churchtown, preceded by the St Day and Chacewater bands, with appropriate banners. After their return, tea was provided for all in a field belonging to Mr R Garland."*

The Band of Hope banner which was bright red in colour

It was the St Day and Redruth bands that provided the music the following year for the procession to Churchtown and then to Trevaunance Pier to take part in the old custom of a penny boat trip. Ashley Rowe concludes by saying, *"I doubt if many villages could now indulge in the luxury of engaging two bands."*

The Revd W Haslam, Vicar of Baldhu, visited Mount Hawke in 1852 and later wrote, *"Here on the appointed Saturday afternoon I found no fewer than 3,000 people assembled on the Common, they had erected a kind of platform with a canvas awning to shelter me from the wind. There I stood and beheld the concourse of people evidently full of eager expectation. I gave out the hymn 'Oh for a thousand tongues to sing, my Great Redeemer's praise,' this was heartily sung and after prayer I announced my text: 'Christ Jesus came into the world to save sinners.' I pressed the thought and a mighty power of the Spirit of the Lord came on the people. It was quite impossible to go on preaching. After about an hour someone suggested that we should go to the schoolroom as it was get-*

ting dark." This was the old Congregational chapel mentioned earlier in this chapter and described in greater detail in the section on the church.

"The clergyman of the parish was in the lane watching proceedings. I asked him if we could have the use of the schoolroom, 'Oh yes,' he replied, 'certainly, certainly, anything.' He seemed very frightened. When I reached the place I found it impossible to get in for it was already full besides a throng standing at the doors. I was taken to a window at last and got in through that. Against the wall men had, after miner's fashion, set up with clay, some candles which were beginning to bend over with the heat of the room. I left at 10 o'clock and the meeting continued all night and all the next day without cessation. That same meeting was prolonged without any intermission day or night till the evening of Sunday, the eighth day after it began."

John Cock was a local preacher, the leader of two chapel classes and a tireless worker for the Wesleyan society. His sudden death in 1887 is recorded as a severe blow to the chapel.

Circa 1903...The tea-treat complete with fairground attractions and brass band

In 1903 there must have been hours of discussion on one particular matter. Despite promises to the contrary, Mount Hawke Wesleyans had decided to renovate their church rather than build a new one. It took several meetings to arrive at this decision and the parties were so evenly divided that it needed the casting vote of the chairman. (RCG 2/4/1903)

But then, in a remarkable about turn, it was to be a new chapel after all with the estimated cost at between £1,000 and £1,200. Plans were put in place to raise the money but the first setback was the contribution from the 20th Century Fund which was to be only £100. There was to be further disappointment when it was discovered that the Connectional Chapel Committee would only provide a similar sum. (RCG August1903) Raising sufficient funds was going to be a problem.

For whatever reason, probably finance, the scheme was back in the melting pot and it was decided that Mount Hawke would not have its new chapel. Instead, the front façade would be re-built, the building renovated and new seats installed. In 1906 Mr Moyle of Chacewater commenced the work for a contract price of £700.

At this time a new board of trustees was appointed: Henry Cocks, Edward Rodda, William Tonkin, John L Williams, Henry Tonkin, Francis Harris, John Goyne, Alfred Tremewan, William J Plummer, Peter Varker, James Tyack, William H Richards, Robert Nicholas, Baiton S Rickeard, Edgar Richards, R R Nancarrow, Arthur Goyne and Thomas Northcott.

Alteration work in progress

The Band of Hope had grown in strength in many communities including at Mount Hawke. Charles Harris presided over a meeting in November 1911 when Ada Vincent, Winnie Tallack, Ivy Matthews, Miss G Rodda,

Miss W Tallack, Reggie Vincent and E Rodda sang. Miss L Stoddern, Myrtle, Ivy, and Louie Matthews and Amy Rodda provided recitations, Stanley Bennett led the choir and Mr R Rodda and Mr J E Oates lectured on the affects of alcohol on the human body. (RCG 23/11/11)

Circa 1910…The interior of the chapel

Will Jones recalled the chapel choir with many excellent singers but he hated his job of pumping the organ. He said, *"On one occasion I pumped for so long that I could hardly stand up."*

The 1920 booklet informs us that the building was illuminated with the *Litz gas* system, the first chapel in Cornwall to use it. Low-pressure hot-water pipes were used to keep the place warm and there was a good two-manual organ, for which, it seems, there had always been an honorary Organist. The Society was almost free from debt.

The booklet continued, *"The Trustees, who are fully alive to the needs of the hour, work assiduously on behalf of the young people. There is a flourishing and well-attended Sunday school, Band of Hope and Wesley Guild and it is hoped that those younger members of the congregation who have the welfare of the church at heart will volunteer their services and come forward with suggestions which will enable that work to be more fully developed. We cannot afford to relax any effort on behalf of the young. The times are full of promise as well as difficulty, the world today is paying in full the price of sin and nothing but the religion of Jesus Christ will save it from worse disaster.*

Let us then fare forth in the strength of our Master with stronger determination than ever, that, as we enter upon the second century in the life of this church, it shall be, not in century old decrepitude but in the exuberance of youth."

John Kinsman, in *The Cornish Handbook*, refers to the Whitsuntide festival in Cornwall when maidens and youths selected it as the season for the display of new clothes. He said, *"Many villages held their 'Tea Drinking' on Whit-Monday. It was the time for lovers to walk together and to indicate their preferences to their neighbours. A 'Tea Drinking' is essentially a social function, enabling all who take part to dispense with the formalities which would keep them apart. First of all, a procession is formed, headed by a brass band and resplendent with banners and flags. After parading the village, it enters a field, lent for the occasion by a friendly farmer and men, women and children sit down to eat huge quantities of saffron cake and drink freshly-made tea, the adults at long tables and the children on seats arranged to form a complete circle. Each child brings his or her own 'Tea Drinking' cup, which is emblazoned with some suitable motto; the tea is poured from huge earthenware pitchers, while saffron cakes are served from wide wicker baskets, each child receiving a whole cake. After tea, music and games fill the hours. The custom is so full of gladness that one hopes it may never be forgotten."*

John wrote this around 1920. Occasionally we hear of one still being held or resurrected but they are now few and far between, a relic of the past.

Claude Tonkin was born at Banns in 1928, in a cottage close to the river. He lived in the village until he was ten or eleven and later returned to raise his family. His recollections are of everyone attending the tea-treats, whether or not they were connected with the chapel. There were all sorts of competitions including the slow bicycle race, fruit sellers, brass band and, of course, the famous tea-treat buns. As Claude said, *"They were, ansum."*

Memories of the procession route are a bit hazy but according to Mary and Donald George it left the chapel and headed out to Short Cross (the junction of Short Cross Road and the Porthtowan road), it then doubled back and continued down the hill to Banns where it paused for a while before heading back to the allotted field. A brave old walk for the players with the largest brass instrument.

Circa 1904...The tea-treat parade coming up through the village led by the banner and the band

Circa 1904...Members of the chapel follow the band

Circa 1910…The tea-treat parade pauses at Banns

Circa 1910…Listening to the band outside the chapel

Circa 1908 … Enjoying the huge tea-treat buns (note the wonderful array of hats) …
Maude Jones and two of her children are on the right

1915 … a typical tea with the best china, trestle tables decorated with flowers and everyone in their
Sunday best. Evelyn Gribben is standing on the left.

A tea-treat egg & spoon race... Miss Dorothy Kinsman (2nd left) with Gladys Richards
(later Gladys Simmons) on her left

During a particular dry spell two people decided to set off for the chapel to pray for rain. It must have been a true sceptic that observed, *"It didn't show much promise, neither one of them had enough faith to carry an umbrella."*

Hayle Band were on duty at the tea-treat in July 1931 and led the parade around the village before returning to a field loaned by Mr E Rodda, probably where *Greenacres* now stands.

Camborne Junior Band was a force to be reckoned with in brass band circles and in 1934 it travelled the short distance to Mount Hawke to provide the musical entertainment at the tea-treat. (RCG 1/8/34)

Richard (Dick) Rodda was a choir member and his niece, Mary, still has his 1935/1936 Mount Hawke Wesley Guild Programme. Listed in it are the names of the officers, committee, organists, readers and perhaps most important of all, the person responsible for lighting the fire.

Hayle Band was back again in 1935 but this year the tea was served in Mr James' field. (RCG 17/7/1935)

This list of organists dates from the early part of the 20th century. We cannot confirm that it is complete or totally accurate but on the basis that these people served their chapel well we have included it. Samuel Rodda (-1919), Millie Thomas, Stanley Bennetts (1920-1925), Harry Carveth

(1923-1930), Mr Trounce, Mr Matthews, Winnifred May (1930-1946), Doreen Hawke (1931-1938), Phyllis Roberts (1931-1936), Mrs Carter, Lettie Strongman (1945-1958), Carrie Yelland (1950-1970), John Townley (1972-1975), Nancy Goyne (1959-2003), Alan Butterfield (1987-   ) and Paula Crook.

Circa 1900...possibly Samuel Rodda

Monty Rodda had an excellent voice; he had been offered a position with the Doyly Carte Opera Company but turned it down. John Jotcham recalled the story of when he was receiving rapturous applause for his rendition of *Old Man River*. A voice from the back said, *"Never mind 'bout encore, let's hear n again."* John also told us a dubious story about a preacher sounding forth about Moses striking the stone and bringing forth water when he noticed some girls giggling. In an attempt to admonish them he said, *"It's all very well for you girls to sit there laughing but you couldn't make water if you tried."*

A regular feature for the men was to round off the Sunday activities with a walk out to the railway halt and back. Gladys Thomas (née Johns) recalled the group which included Howard Chynoweth, George Tallack and his brother, Jack. Gladys also remembered *seat rent,* the payment of a quarterly sum to reserve a pew, and woe betide anyone else who tried to use it. It seems that the decision to make all seats free caused quite a stir in chapel circles with one or two taking advantage of the situation by deliberately sitting in seats previously *owned* by others.

Circa 1950…The chapel with its 1906 façade

1950…The band play outside Mr James' shop for the tea-treat celebrations

Gladys Thomas was Trust Secretary in the 1950s and very involved in the various events. She said, *"We held our Christmas Market on Boxing Day, you wouldn't think people would turn up but they did. There were all types of stalls… laid out in the Sunday school."*

Harvest Festival was a major celebration which took many days of preparation. Wednesday and Thursday was spent in arranging the goods including, as Gladys said, *"Bunching up the corn."* Friday was the day for decorating the chapel; the *Faith Tea* was on the Saturday followed by a talk, usually on the theme of Harvest. Sunday was a full day of celebration with morning and evening services. Monday was the fun day with the auction of fruit and vegetables.

Concerts by the Goonhavern Banjo Band were always popular; who could forget the inimitable Glen Pedlar, and in what must have been a major event in 1926 Madame Jessie Strathearn ARAM (London) entertained with her talks and songs.

Gladys' mother was Evelyne Ernestine Johns (née Cole) who was also involved in chapel life. After her first husband, Sidney, died she married Norman Dell, a familiar figure around the village.

Following the renovation of the organ a service of re-dedication was held on the 28th March 1990 when the Revd Steven Emery-Wright and the Revd Ian Haile officiated. It featured the Goonvrea Singers and David Briggs, Organist and Master of the Choristers at Truro Cathedral.

A number of people have mentioned Bryanites Corner, at the junction of the Banns and the Porthtowan road. It seems that there was a Bible Christian or Bryanite Chapel located there and we have found some evidence to support this on early maps.

For many people, life revolved around the chapel; that was the way it was in rural communities. Youngsters involved themselves in the services, the Sunday school and the social events; it was a major part of their life. It is less so today and there are many who believe that communities are poorer because of it.

The Church

In 1845 the government introduced the Church Extension Act, this authorised the creation of many new parishes. By this the ecclesiastical parish of Mount Hawke came into being, formed from parts of Perranzabuloe and Illogan.

The following year these new ecclesiastical districts were formally established as described in this Schedule Order in Council dated 6th July 1846. The first incumbent at Mount Hawke was in place by the 3rd February 1847.

The District of Mount Hawke being:

> All that part of the Chapelry of Saint Agnes, in the County of Cornwall, and in the Diocese of Exeter, situate on the Western side of an imaginary line extending Southward from the Northern boundary of the said Chapelry at Chapel Porth, along a certain rivulet known by the name of Mingoose River, to the corner of Bann's Estate, and thence in a straight direction towards the South-West to Towan Cross, and thence towards the South-East, along the middle of the main road leading into the turnpike road from St Agnes to Truro, as far as Mingoose Barrow, and thence towards the South-West, along the Eastern boundary of a certain estate called Trevithick, to the South-Eastern corner thereof, and thence also, towards the South-West, and in a straight direction to the North-Eastern corner of the Goosewarra Estate, and thence in a like direction to the North-Western corner of a certain field now in the occupation of Richard Truran, and numbered 3,056 on the parish map of Saint Agnes, and thence Southward along the middle of a certain road leading to Edward's Brewery at Blackwater, as far as the Southern boundary of the said Chapelry of Saint Agnes; and also all that part of the Parish of Illogan, in the same county and diocese, situate on the Eastern side of an imaginary line extending Northward from the boundary between the said Parish of Illogan and the Parish of Redruth, in the same county and diocese, along the Western fence or boundary of the estate called Kite's Enclosure, across the high road to Portreath, and along the middle of a certain

road or lane leading to Fiddle Bottom, and thence towards the
North-West along a certain small stream or rivulet to the North-
Western boundary of the said Parish of Illogan at Kerrier Cove.

In his series of articles for the *West Briton* in 1958, Ashley Rowe wrote about
the curious feature of the Extension movement of 1846 whereby incumbents were appointed to the new districts and left to make their own arrangements for building a church and vicarage. They were given a free hand
but that seemed to be the only thing they were given.

A disused Congregational chapel in Old Church Lane was borrowed and
put to use as a church and schoolroom. An old St Agnes guidebook refers
to it as *the old church in the field* and in 1852 the Revd Haslam used it after
an open-air service (revival meeting). Some notes passed to us suggest that
both its windows and roof were round and that its final use was as a barn.
In 1958 Ashley Rowe said that it was still possible to trace fragments of the
path that led to it.

The Revd E M Hamilton, the first incumbent of Mount Hawke in 1847,
continued to use the old building while trying to raise money for something
more adequate but, by the time of his death in 1862, little progress had been
made. In the following 12 years there were no less than five incumbents;
Henry Stone, who only remained one year, W H Brenton appointed in 1863,
William Avery in 1868, Isodore Dampre in 1871, who resigned in 1873
and the fifth, William Henry Allin, a resolute character who was destined to
make a difference.

The living was in the gift of the Crown and Bishop alternately but owing
to the difficulty in finding a candidate, the right of presentation lapsed and it
was the Archbishop of Canterbury who appointed the Revd W H Allin.

He was a Devonshire man and before coming to Mount Hawke had
been a curate at Stonehouse and at Christ Church, Plymouth. He remained
at Mount Hawke for five years, then left to become Vicar of St Mary's,
Devonport. During those five years he accomplished what had seemed an
impossible task … the building of the church.

Some of the early incumbents had made attempts to raise the necessary
funds but had given up in despair and when the Reverend Allin was appointed there was only £20 in the building fund and hardly any congregation.

He was a formidable and tenacious man; he rebuilt the congregation and
set about the task of erecting a place of worship. The church logbook states,

"*Through Mr Allin, by his letters, sermons and appeals in various forms, the benighted condition of Mount Hawke, as far as the church was concerned, was made known throughout the length and breadth of Cornwall and even beyond, and by persistent requests and appeals he gathered sufficient funds to erect a church.*"

The church was built close to the road, near Shortcross, and although the funds were limited, too limited for much ornamentation, the building was said to be substantial and built of the best materials.

Mr E W Brydges Willyams of Carnanton gave the land for the church and for the vicarage and schoolroom which were built a little later. Prior to that the Vicar lived at Mingoose.

c. 1930...The Church with its schoolroom and vicarage

When in August 1878 the *West Briton* reported the opening of the new church it said, "*Our readers must be familiar with the subject of Mount Hawke Church but the thing which was a shadow has now become substance.*

Mount Hawke is a considerable village, near St Agnes, rarely approached by strangers and it has no inn at which they might be refreshed, nor has it any particular natural attraction which would tempt the traveller to go out of his way to visit it, but it has a population, whose souls have to be cared for. The Church, however, as has been its wont in Cornwall, in years gone by, neglected the people, and Methodism took the place which the Church ought to have held."

The report referred to the large, comfortable Methodist Chapel and to the fact that the church had previously hired a place that was little better than a barn which brought ridicule upon them.

The church was completed by August 1878 at a cost of £1,200 and the Revd Allin was credited not only for its construction but also for building a congregation and a Sunday school of 40 children, in the space of only four years.

Local historian Ashley Rowe was clearly not impressed with the actual building which he described as having no claim to any architectural or aesthetic value. He said that it was severely plain and entirely devoid of ornament and if a name must be given to the style he would describe it as Early English. *"It consists of a nave and chancel only, with a vestry at the east and a porch on the west end of the south side. There is a small bell turret at the west end of the building. It was definitely a case of cutting one's coat according to the cloth. It has, however, the merit of being a local production; the architect was Charles Hancock of St Agnes and the builders were Mitchell and Langdon, also of St Agnes, together with Tamblyn of Redruth.*

Until comparatively recent years (written in 1958) there were people living in Mount Hawke who were proud to say their fathers had helped build the church."

The interior of the Church

The building stone came from a quarry at Croft Prince, it has granite plinths, angles and corbels and Bath stone dressings for the windows and doors. The alley and chancel are laid with Bridgewater black and red tiles.

The Bishop of Truro, Dr E W Benson, consecrated and dedicated the new church to St John the Baptist on the 5th August 1878, this was the first church to be consecrated by him and the first new church in the restored Diocese of Truro.

Ashley Rowe continued, *"The ceremony took place on a Bank Holiday but such days were then but little regarded in rural districts and the attendance was neither more nor less because of it. Cornish villages in particular maintained their own holidays, the parish feasts, Mount Hawke long observed St Agnes feast and the fair days, their own if they had one, or those of the nearest town. Bank holidays, as such, were very slowly recognised."*

That August day the church was packed. The clergy present included the Archdeacon, W J Phillpotts, Canon A J Mason as the Bishop's Chaplain, plus many vicars from neighbouring parishes. The proceedings commenced at 11.00 am, the form of consecration being that used in the diocese of Exeter.

The procession of the clergy was met at the church by a parishioner, A J Hitchens, who presented the petition to the Bishop praying for the consecration of the church … it was signed by William Henry Allin, John Opie, John Hitchins, Edward Jeffery, Robert Williams, Francis James, William Mitchell and R J Menadue.

The Bishop accepted the petition and responded: *"I beseech God, bless and prosper the good work we are going about."*

At this time the church did not possess an organ but apparently a young chap called Williams, the son of the schoolmistress, played a harmonium.

The Bishop stayed for the public luncheon in the village schoolroom and apparently teased Mr Allin on his persistence; he had had to cancel his holiday to be there. He said that he had been there a year before to lay the church foundation stone and he supposed he would have to come again to lay the foundation stone of a tower and then for a peal of bells. Ashley Rowe commented that these promised visits had not yet become necessary.

The *West Briton* concluded its report of the event by saying, *"Mr Allin thanked all his kind friends who had given him such willing aid during the time he had been in the district. When he came there were only one or two communicants and now he had a considerable congregation; friends in the village had even contributed the luncheon. He had pleaded the cause in nearly 40 churches from Camborne to Plymouth and Falmouth."*

The church logbook records that this was Wilson Langdon's first building contact. It seems that when preparing his tender for the work he had overlooked the porch. When he had spoken to Mr Allin about it he was, *"… as usual, very nice and most amicable arrangements were made."*

Unfortunately it was not long before dry rot was discovered and work was necessary to eradicate it … a problem also experienced at St Agnes Church.

The Vicarage was built in the Reverend Dungey's time, at a cost of £560. The logbook records a dispute between the builder, the architect and the Building Committee. *"Lawyers were called in and it cost the Building Committee, judging from the bills still in the parish safe, more than £100. James Julian of Truro was the architect and apparently his bill was more than £50. The building of the Vicarage is said to be very defective and in one way and another it cost a large sum. Towards this, Queen Ann's Bounty gave £500. Another £300 was taken from the capital of the benefice in Mr Stona's time and spent in alterations about the Vicarage."*

Mr Dungey also built the schoolroom, in 1881, but most of the furniture was said to be of poor quality having been taken from the old church. The logbook records, *"New trestles and planks have been secured for the platform and also a new case for frontals and cups and saucers and plates etc. For the conveyance of a little extra land for the Sunday school Mr Dungey paid £120. The room was found to be too small to meet the needs of the parish and in 1904 Mr Rodda enlarged it at a cost of about £80."*

The Church and schoolroom

Wilson Langdon installed a bell for a cost of £10.2.2 and the Alms box was presented by Captain John and Mrs Rogers of *Wingfield*, the wood having come from India.

The font was provided by Coulter Hancock of the Manor Office, St Agnes, with the comments, *"The Font now in your church formerly belonged to the chapel of the mansion at Trevaunance. This mansion was very large containing more than 100 rooms. It had a flat roof and a private chapel was served by a resident priest... the family being Roman Catholics. In the troublous times it was the hiding place of fugitive priests and tradition states that King Charles II was also sheltered there. The grounds were of great extent, including a large woods, a deer park... the wall of this can now be traced in Rocky Lane and other places... fishponds etc. The Font was lent to the first vicar of Mount Hawke for the old church. When the new church was built the Font was presented to it by the Lords of Trevaunance. The architect had the font re-cut thus removing the delicate* tracery and the remains of the Coat of Arms in fact, destroying all traces of its origin." (A comment initialled WF states, "A very great pity indeed; they must have been mad.")

The Reverend Stona installed a new altar rail, made by Gill of Truro, new candlesticks, the lectern, hangings and large lamps. He also had a new bell made out of the existing cracked bell and the one from the old church.

The logbook states, "*The marble monument in the north wall and the corona with three lamps in the chancel were placed there by devoted parishioners to commemorate the good work and saintly life of Mr Dungey.*" It also states, "*The following additions have been added during Mr Barfett's time: the organ has been got, the new oak lectern which has been procured by the kindness of Miss Sandoe who collected the funds for it, the new brass plate erected to the memory of the lamented Mr Allin, the new tiled floor with granite altar steps erected to the memory of the Argall family by Miss Jane Argall… new cross for altar which cost £7 collected by Miss Barfett, new violet alms bags made and given by Mrs Phillips of Skinners Bottom, new white alms bags presented with book markers by Miss Holloway, new trestles and wood for the school platform, a new box for cleaning materials and another for linen, a new case for the frontals, a new fire-proof safe and a new clock in the vestry. The Bishop's chair was given in 1908 by the dining students of South Kensington School of Mines, a new chalice veil was given by Miss Vine of Penryn, a new lace for the alter was given by Miss Scewes of Truro, two new lamps were given by Mr and Mrs Tilly of The Glen, new violet frontals and hangings for the prayers books and pulpit were also very kindly given by Mr and Mrs Tilly.*"

By 1876 the churchyard and the cemetery at St Agnes were too small to serve the needs of the parish and in the following year a cemetery was created at Mount Hawke, on the land adjacent to the new church. This was placed under the control of St Agnes Burial Board.

The cemetery is divided into two sections, the western half being consecrated according to the rites of the Church of England. A gateway connects it with the church grounds and this is only used on the occasion of burials. In 1902 the St Agnes Burial Board made an effort to build up the gateway between the graveyard and the church but it was strongly opposed. After producing proof of a right of way the Board gave in.

Circa 1900...The access gate between the Church and graveyard

A group of Church members in 1905/6... Richard Menadue is to the left of Vicar John Ching Barfett

A granite Celtic cross stands at the entrance to the graveyard, erected as a memorial to the fallen in the 1914-18 war; the names of those who died in the 1939-45 war have since been added.

The Methodist tea-treats were open to the entire village but the church also had its teas although perhaps not on the same scale.

The Coronation of King George V in 1911 was celebrated with a united service in the church and afterwards the congregation enjoyed a public tea in a nearby field. There were sports, a baby show and the distribution of commemorative mugs. The logbook recorded, *"There was a large bonfire in Mr James Rodda's hill. Everything went off most harmoniously."*

In 1911 the colour of the church walls were changed from red to green and a copper cowl was placed on the flue. On the 4th October 1913 a Special Vestry Meeting was held to appoint a new People's Warden, Mr J Robbins had moved away and Mr T Tymes was appointed to take his place, sworn in by the Bishop of St Germans.

The Sunday school prize distribution on the 7th January 1915 was described in the logbook as, *"A happy meeting."* It was, no doubt, some respite from the news of the war.

In his written address to parishioners in March 1915 the Revd Beecroft referred to the Tresavean Mine disaster in which 32 year-old William Ewart Bennetts died.

An extract from the vicar's diary states, *"On the 14th April 1915, at a meeting of the Parishioners, it was agreed to form an Electoral Roll of all communicants and regular worshippers at the church and that as soon as the Roll was completed an election of representative members of the Church Council should take place and that two representatives should be elected from each district of the parish viz. Mount Hawke, Porthtowan and Gooneearl with Skinners Bottom."*

Mrs Daddow died in May 1915, presumably the same lady referred to in the Women's Institute scrapbook which says, *"Mrs Daddow is remembered by her strange request to be buried lying on her side. Mr Gribben who helped to make her coffin tells us that this request was fulfilled."*

In 1916 there was reference to The Girl's Club. This met on Saturday evenings and in February of the following year the Young Women's Guild performed the *Operetta Genevieve*.

Later that year it was considered that new church gates were required and a collection was started.

In 1918 the *Carnmarth Deanery Magazine* was discontinued and an attempt to produce a Mount Hawke Parish Magazine was proposed but dropped due to the cost involved.

In October 1927 a dance was held to raise money for the church lighting scheme. (RCG 12/10/1927) As things turned out it was Mrs Williams of Redruth who paid for the installation; the new lights must have made life considerably easier.

Gertrude Rodda was the organist but it seems that this may never have been the case had she been allowed to play at the chapel where her brother Richard (Dick) was a staunch choir member. She was also a sister to Ernest and Edgar Rodda.

The Reverend Ward and his family are fondly remembered although, perhaps, a little eccentric. They had one son, George, who became an actor and appeared in several productions, in the Ealing Comedies and the *Carry on* films. Apparently it was well known that if the family were invited to tea they would clear everything on the table, not a crumb would be left. *"But then,"* said Chris Chynoweth, *"that was before my time."*

The fancy dress dance competition in February 1931 produced some interesting costumes and a considerable amount of fun. It was held in the church hall and Miss Barkle and Mrs M Hicks took first prize for the best couple with their Venetian boatmen. The Mordaunt Orchestra provided the music and Mr Conquest was the Master of Ceremonies. (RCG 4/2/1931)

The Reverend Greaves moved to Mount Hawke in 1939 and within a short time his wife died. Miss Phyllis Benham had been involved in church activities for some time and in due course she became the second Mrs Greaves. There was clearly a lot of affection for the Reverend Greaves. Monty Burrows remembers his cousins being allowed to go to the vicarage for a bath. He said, *"That was the sort of person he was."*

The Choir in the 1940s during the Reverend Greaves' incumbency
(L to R) Miss Benham (later Mrs Greaves), Mrs Eslick, Gertrude Rodda, (Mary Rodda's aunt),
Miss Rodgers (Miss Benham's cousin), Mrs Tippett and Mrs Frost (source Mary Rodda)

The following stories were conveyed with a plea for anonymity that bordered on desperation and a fear of excommunication. They all relate to activities in or near the church hall, about sixty years ago. Let's just say that a group of lads were gathered outside; one of the windows was partly open providing ventilation to the whist players; Mrs Strike was shuffling the cards. It was November and like good Protestant boys they were intent on celebrating the glorious fifth. One of them happened to have a *Jumping Jack* handy, a firework that has now been banned on safety grounds. He lit it and threw it through the window. With great presence of mind the lively Mrs Strike dropped the cards, picked up the offending, and ready to detonate, banger and threw it back through the window… at the feet of the fast-disappearing boys. The determination of youth knows no bounds and the *Little-demon* banger, placed in a key-hole of the entrance door, was ample compensation for the failure of the first ploy. It required an urgent call to a carpenter to replace the timber lock block of the entrance door. I'm not sure if it was the same evening but Russell Pearce from Manor Parsley (see, he mentioned his name) clambered onto the roof and placed a piece of slate over a smoking chimney pot. The resultant melee needs no description.

Cyril Martin probably regretted his bold claim of having no fear of ghosts when Francis Garland, complete with white sheet, suddenly appeared before him in the graveyard. It was a while before he stopped running.

Health and Safety didn't exist in the 1950s and when Archie Pheby pulled the rope to ring the bell he must have noticed a change in tension... the bell had fallen off. Miss Hoadley was walking by at the time and must have been extremely surprised, and not a little shaken, to find that it had just missed her. It was many years before it was replaced and a plaque on the wall tells us that a new one was presented during the late 1960s in memory of Reginald Herbert Russell of Porthtowan. The call to church could resume.

Circa 1950... The Church choir

The Nativity Play in the 1950s (photo Ken Young)

Chris Chynoweth had a couple of tales of near disaster, the first was just a few years ago, at Rogationtide in the Spring, when the crops are blessed. He said, *"At Evensong we would process into the fields for part of the service. Having completed the route the procession filed back into the church led by the server swinging the incense thurible. On reaching the chancel it hit the step flinging the red-hot charcoal everywhere. The choir, who were following, suddenly broke into a war dance as they tried to stamp out the hot embers. Having ground them into the carpet they solemnly filed into their pews and the service was completed.*

Another near disaster was during Advent when a large wreath was suspended from the roof truss. It was on a pulley mechanism so that it could be lowered to light the candles. This was done with all due ceremony.

Suddenly there was a loud crackling sound; the greenery around the candles had burst into flames. The wreath was hurriedly lowered and the fire extinguisher brought into play. Luckily there was not much harm and the service continued."

It was said that the cessation of mining led to the reduction in the population in some of the parishes but for whatever reason congregations were reducing and Mount Hawke and Mithian were combined into a united benefice in 1958. When the Revd F N Greaves retired the new incumbent took charge of both parishes. The two areas had been independent for more than a century having been formed as *Peel districts,* created under the Church Extension Act introduced by Sir Robert Peel.

It was a Charles Dickens theme for the 1984 annual market when the best costume award was presented to Mrs Dorcas Shipman who was Madam Mantolini from Nicholas Nickleby.

The Curates, Vicars and Priests in charge across the years.

1847 to 1862   Edward Montague Hamilton presented by the Queen.

1862 to 1863   Henry Stone presented by the Bishop.

1863 to 1868   Henry Wheeler Brenton presented by the Queen.

1868 to 1871   William Avery presented by the Bishop.

1871 to 1874   Isidore Daimpre presented by the Queen.

1874 to 1878   William Henry Allin presented by the Archbishop of Canterbury by reason of lapse. It was in his time the Parish Church was built.
He is listed as the first Incumbent (Vicar).

1879 to 1891   John Dungey presented by the Queen.

1891 to 1900   John Stona presented by the Bishop.

1900 to 1914   John Ching Barfett presented by the Queen.

1914 to 1923   John Henry James Peter Beecroft presented by the Bishop of Truro.

1923 to 1927   William Fookes presented by the King (George VI).

1927 to 1933   Philip John Coleman

1933 to 1939   William George Henry Ward

1939 to 1958   Francis Neville Greaves

1958 to 1961   Ronald Jack Edmondson

1961 to 1977   Sydney Thomas Craddock. Following the Revd Craddock's retirement the Bishop suspended the presentation which meant that he would not, for the moment, accept the appointment of a new vicar in the full legal sense.

1977 to 1979   John George Stunden (Priest in charge)

1979 to 1984   John Tredinnick officiated pending new appointment.

1984 to 1990   Clifford James Hankins

1990 to 1995   Peter Woodhall

1995 to 1999   Michael John Adams (Priest in charge)

Revd Derek Hollingdale assisted and officiated pending new appointment.

2001   Alan George Bashforth
2003 to 2006   Revd Hilary Samson assisted.

The differences between chapel and church hymnbooks were highlighted at one ecumenical service some years ago when the hymn number was announced but, unlike the custom at chapel, the first line was not read out. It was to be *Guide me O thou Great Redeemer*. In the chapel book however it states *Jehovah* and not *Redeemer*. Everyone struck up and one chapel person, obviously singing the words from memory, lustily sang out the name *Jehovah*. The church lady in front turned around and in an equally loud voice said, *"We don't 'ave 'ee up 'ere."*

Chris Chynoweth is a Church Warden, his father, Harry, also held this post for almost 40 years and his great grandfather, Richard Menadue, was the Church Parish Clerk when the church was being built. Chris recalled an item from an old service register lodged at the County Records Office; an amusing entry by his great grandfather, Richard Menadue, the church Parish Clerk. It highlights the comparative value of money a hundred years ago. Chris said he had entered the collection takings into the book as he was supposed to do but in the column alongside he had written a note, *"Mr Menadue put in half a crown (12.5p) by mistake, took out 1/6d. (7.5p)."*

It was change again in 1995 when St Agnes was joined with Mount Hawke and Mithian to became an even larger united benefice. The vicar continued to be referred to as the Priest in charge and it was not until the Reverend Alan Bashforth was appointed that the change was fully formalised.

The School

Prior to 1870 many children received no education and those that did were taught at home or in private or church schools. We referred earlier to the use of the old congregational chapel as both a church and schoolroom and it is quite possible that it was also a day school. No doubt there were other schools in the village; there is a reference to one opening in 1865 and the Cornwall Trade Directory lists James Nettle as a schoolmaster in 1856 and 1862. Richard John Menadue was said to have run a school; he was a great grandfather of Joan and Chris Chynoweth.

The Elementary Education Act of August 1870 introduced Board Schools throughout England and Wales. It caused controversy in some homes as many felt that people ought to provide for themselves while others despaired at the loss of cheap labour in the mines and on the farms. In 1880 education became compulsory for children up to ten years old but, even then, it was not free.

Ashley Rowe wrote that in 1874 the St Agnes School Board accepted plans for a school at Mount Hawke and a contract was placed with John Bone and Son of Liskeard to build it at a cost of £1,129. It was to be for 250 children but this was later reduced to 200, probably by the removal of a gallery in the largest room.

In his book *Friendly Retreat*, Maurice Bizley referred to the headmaster who was absent with a serious illness from October 1874 to January 1875; for that period Miss Blight taught both the girls and the boys.

Many parents objected to the loss of their cheap labour and truancy was a problem, particularly at harvest time. The headmaster pressed for the appointment of a school visitor or attendance officer and in April 1875 John Tregea was in that role. (Kelly's Directories 1889 to 1902). It is possible that he was also the village boot and shoemaker. By 1906 Mr A Tremewan of Manor Parsley had taken over with the title of *School Attendance Officer for St Agnes Section of the Redruth & Camborne Education Committee.*

Shortly after the headmaster recorded, *"This week has been characterised by the influx of several boys who previous to the appointment of a Visitor appeared to have been going to no school whatever and hence were literally doing nothing. Their attainments are nil and, consequently, a separate preparatory class has been made."*

From February 1876 grammar and geography were compulsory subjects and the School Board decided to provide home lesson books for the children. Francis James was the headmaster, or master, and it was not long before an assistant mistress for the infants department was appointed.

By 1887 the school had been running for a dozen years or so, it had been accepted into the community and many children had passed through its hands, in some cases reluctantly. Imagine then the consternation at the sudden death of its youthful headmaster. Francis James was only 37 and seemingly in good health but a sudden pain in his side made him seek medical help. It was not considered serious but within two days he was dead.

The West Briton recorded, *"In the Wesleyan Chapel, on Sunday, after morning service, the 'Dead March from Saul' was played on the organ by the chapel organist, Mr A Walters, the congregation standing. Many seemed entirely unable to conceal their sorrowful emotions."*

At his funeral he was described as a zealous churchman who was respected by everyone in the village. Following the service the procession of a hearse and 16 carriages wound its way to the churchyard at Carnmenellis.

By 1889 the average attendance at the school was 45 boys, 40 girls and 20 infants. Miss Hampton was the infants' teacher; described in the mid 1890s as an elderly lady. Edgar Richards was the headmaster; he was assiduous in his efforts to achieve good attendance as portrayed by Eddie Tredinnick in the 8th Journal of the St Agnes Museum Trust. Eddie attended Mount Hawke School for a while, following the closure of St Agnes School during a diphtheria epidemic. His account describes how boys often ran away to follow the hounds. *"Once Master, as he was generally known, came after them. Of course, they had to return to school and had the cane. At the end of term they broke up at dinnertime but some of the boys again used to try and run off at playtime, about 11 o'clock. Again, Master came after them on his bicycle but they dodged into the fields to avoid him, thinking that he would not remember their actions for three weeks. However, on the first day of the next term they were called out and given the cane."*

Edgar Richards was born at Mawla, on his father's farm and met his future wife at the school where she was a pupil teacher; they lived and started their family at Menagissey.

As headmaster he would have been an important and influential member of the community and from what we have found it is clear that he had a profound affect of the early years of the school which by then had grown to 120 pupils.

The School of 1898

Circa 1900…Children posing for the photographer

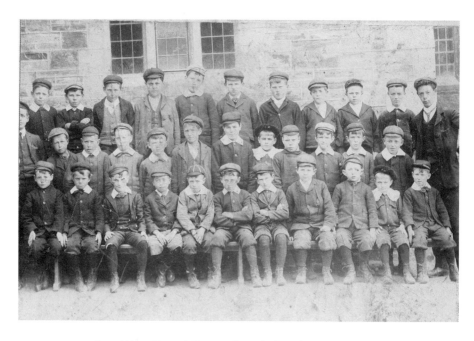

Circa 1902... Howard Chynoweth on the far right is a pupil teacher

In 1908 Edgar Richards was successful in gaining a teaching position at the Oliver Goldsmith's School and, with his family, left Cornwall for a new challenge. Within a couple of years they had a daughter, Audrey (later Foster) and it was from her daughter, Wendy Norris, that we received this information.

Over the years Edgar and his family made regular return visits to Cornwall, Audrey, now 98 years of age, remembers them with great happiness.

Ernest Landry attended the school during the very early 1900s and in *Memories of Nancekuke*, he wrote, *"I rather enjoyed going there, I had plenty of company with the coastguards' children. Walking from Porthtowan we used to take our dinner to the school and having an hour and a half for dinner, we used to go to Gover Valley where there was a stream with several trout. When the stream was running low we used to drive them beneath the stones and catch them with our hands. It didn't matter very much if we returned a bit late, providing we had one or two to give to the schoolmaster."*

Circa 1904... Playtime and once again the children pose for the photographer

Joseph Radcliffe was the Master in 1911 but clearly all was not well as this item shows. *"St Agnes managers of the Council schools met on Thursday, Mr John Hitchens J P presiding, to appoint headmasters to Mount Hawke and Mithian Schools, vacated by the removal of Mr J Radcliffe (Mount Hawke) and the lamentable death of Mr J E Tremewan...*

The County Council sent down six names from which to make the selection and after the candidates had been interviewed a ballot was taken with the result that Mr Roskrow was appointed to the Mithian School and Mr Edward James Oates to Mount Hawke." (RCG January 1911)

This picture is from the early 1920s
Back row (L to R): Pearl Tippett, Phyllis Wadge, unknown, ? Mannell, Cora Jones and unknown.
Third row: Includes Bernard Wilkins, Monty Rodda & Ken Bennetts.
Second Row: unknown, unknown, Dorothy James, ? Parsons, ? Tippett, ? Parsons & Iris Carlyon.

Front row: unknown, unknown, Will Carlyon & Georgie James.

Lorna White attended from 1924, when Harry Carveth was headmaster, and recalled two other teachers, Hilda Trelease from Blackwater and Phyllis Berryman from Camborne. Mrs Evelyn Rodda and Harry Chenoweth's wife were involved in organising school concerts in the chapel and church. Lorna said, *"When I was eleven I went to school in Truro and that meant a long walk to the railway halt. There was usually a straight-through train but if the main-line train was late we had to change at Chacewater Station; that was a bleak spot. The walk home from the halt was a bit scary in winter, the woods on the left was full of owls."*

Joan Chynoweth started school in 1927 and recalled teachers Miss Sampson and Mrs Lockett. She said, *"We had a Cornish Range in the infants' classroom, it was where the children warmed their pasties."* By the time that Donald George started school in 1929 Miss Venner was the head teacher.

The class of 1933
Back row (L to R): Ronald Hooper, Joan Chynoweth, Mary George, Lorna Holbeach, Jane Richards, Doreen Nicholls & Courtney Hocking.
Third row: Francis Garland, Russell Pearce, Clifford Holbeach, Barbara Snell, Jo Wonnacott, Owen Fowler, Edgar Pascoe & Donald George.
Second row: Lorna Hocking, Joy Richards, Thelma Leatham, Cecily Jeffrey, Thora Varker & Gladys Martin.
Front row: Brian Reynolds, Claud Pearce, Douglas Tonkin, Gerald Tonkin, Bobbie Fowler, Russell Fowler & Cuthbert Matthews.

Dennis Barbary started his education there in 1938 but had to leave after just three weeks… they closed the school. He was quick to tell us that it wasn't because of him; the numbers had dropped so low that it was no longer considered viable to keep it open.

Writing in the 10th Journal of the St Agnes Museum Trust, Stella Edwards from Gover Hill recalled the closure. *"Mount Hawke School closed and Mr Dale's taxi came from St Agnes to pick up the children to take them to that school."* Gladys Thomas (née Johns) recalled two taxis, one for the boys and one for the girls.

The school re-opened in 1941 to accommodate war evacuees from London. Claude Tonkin had started there in 1933 and recalled the early stages of the Second World War, when the evacuees arrived. He said, *"One of the* punishments for bad behaviour was to stand facing a dividing screen. Claude Jeffrey never liked this and would end up kicking hell out of it. The evacuees arrived complete with their own teachers; one of them was very harsh. I used to think that he hated Cornish kids.

Rex Barkle and his two sisters arrived late one day and were each given the cane and then, just before assembly, they nipped out of the door and ran home. Their father, Johnny, wanted to know what they were doing there and when they wouldn't say he went to see their teacher. Johnny had lost the lower part of an arm in an accident and that sleeve always hung loose at his side. He clearly didn't agree with the teacher as after listening to him for a while he swung the stump of his arm and hit him with his sleeve sending him down for the count."

Gladys Thomas also has unpleasant memories of the teachers who came down from London with the evacuees, particularly Mr Nicholls, the headmaster, who was, "... always very keen to bring out the cane." Lorna Rundle also referred to this gentleman but we decided not to include her comments. Suffice to say that she was not particularly fond of him.

When the evacuees and their teachers returned home after the war the school remained open as a junior school.

Drill sessions sometime around 1948
Includes Maureen Williams (later Townsend), Edwyna Mewton (later Hall), Pauline Pascoe (later Green), Ann Rodda and Marian Stevens

Peter Wilkins attended from 1946 to 1951, when Miss Dawe was the head and Mrs Luff was one of the teachers. He said, *"I remember the old iron stove with a large metal guard around it. That was where we dried our clothes if we were caught in the rain on the way to school. I always enjoyed singing and taking part in the Christmas plays."*

Monty Burrows recalled the stove with bottles of milk placed around it. The one-third of a pint bottles were a feature of school life and in Mount Hawke the children clearly preferred them warm. Monty said, *"I didn't get on with Miss Dawe. I hated semolina and tapioca puddings but she made me eat them … until the day I threw up. I remember Mike Pheby and I making cigarettes and selling them, we'd managed to get some tobacco and papers from somewhere. Thinking about it, there were probably good reasons why Miss Dawe and I didn't get on."*

In September 1948 there were 46 children at the school and in that month two new steaming ovens were delivered, Miss Vanstone was appointed cook and Miss Kinsman her helper. A 20 gallon boiler arrived in January 1949 but try as they might they couldn't get it in through the door.

There were big changes in the provision of school meals in June 1949 as arrangements were put in place for Mount Hawke School to be the location of the Central Kitchen. Miss Vanstone was appointed Supervisor and Miss Paull the cook, assisted by Mrs Lambert. The logbook records that on the 27th June, 493 meals were cooked and sent out to the schools at Blackwater, Chacewater, Penwartha, Mithian and St Agnes. Graham Carlyon recalled that two Ford delivery vans were kept in their garages; Jack Varker was one of the drivers.

The school play in 1950
The names as written on the back of the photograph … regrettably there is one missing:
Peter Wilkins, Tommy Dunstan, David Perry, Simon Perry, Michael Pheby, Monty Burrows,
David Wilkins, David Taylor, Christine Harvey, Jennifer Pascoe, Jean Lambert, Christine Foden,
Julie Foden, Irene Dunstan, Pauline Chatterton & Julie Sleep.

1951 … Physical Education time in the schoolyard

Graham and Sharman Carlyon attended in the 1950s and recall the outside toilet with its high dividing wall; the boys to the right and girls to the left.

In March 1954 the Tortoise Stove in Class III was giving trouble (who could forget the wonderful warmth, and smeech, that came from those old stoves) and in 1955 there were 71 pupils, all between the ages of five and eleven.

Penny O'Keeffe (née Tompkins) attended in the late 1950s although she was not a Mount Hawke girl; she lived on a smallholding around the Beacon. St Agnes was growing and its school was becoming oversubscribed and could not accommodate everyone in its catchment area.

Penny said, *"I grew up accepting that my early years of education would be at Mount Hawke. Harper and Kellow's coach transported about fifty children there each day, to what is now The Old School Pub. The coach was a Bedford Vista with seating for thirty-four adults and to accommodate the numbers three children had to squeeze into the double seats, as the bus company put it, 'three for two.'*

My recollections of the journeys are very vivid. Ronnie Knight was our driver and even to this day he recalls my mother, Betty Tompkins, carrying my school-bag from our home at 'Little Bungay Farm' to meet the coach at the end of the lane. My elder brother, Roger, and I attended there until we transferred to second-ary education.

Our head teacher was Miss Dawe; she was very strict and remained there until her retirement. Mrs Luff, another teacher from St Agnes, was very gentle and made my school days pleasurable.

I have lived in Mount Hawke for the past seventeen years and my children, Callum and Saffron, both attended the new school. In the year 2000 I took a job there and have worked there for the past eight years: something I would never have dreamt of as I travelled there all those years ago. Although I regard myself as being a St Agnes girl, I consider myself lucky to be a Mount Hawke local as well… the best of both worlds."

By 1961 the number of pupils had risen to 111 and a year later, when Mrs Luff was appointed deputy head, to 123.

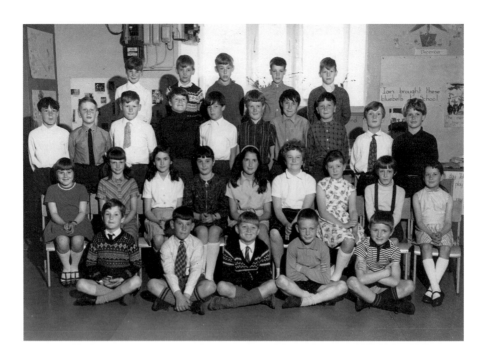

Miss Dawe's class in 1968
Back row (L to R): Chris Wills, Bill Herman, Antony Pain, Andrew Honer & Paul Long.
Third row: Robert Landry, David Dunstan, David Teague, Jonathan Hayter, Alan Jolly,
Kenneth Walker, Paul Thomas, Paul Dudding, Ian Lawrence & Clive Brooks.
Second row: Gillian Swallow, Shirley Carter, Helen Tonkin, Drucilla O'Shea, Annette Barrow,
Sally Newman, Bridgette Philby, Sandra Barkle & Alex Kay.
Front row: Brian Lawrence, Chris Williams, Ian Spurling, Kenneth Wignall & Michael George.
(Names as spelt on rear of photograph)

Mount Hawke School's centenary in 1974 was widely celebrated as the entire village has invited to a service of celebration in Mount Hawke Methodist Church. Headmistress Miss E Dawe had invited the villagers to an open day to see the school at work and the serving of the midday meal. Invitations were sent to all known past scholars, county education staff and school governors. In addition, former pupils over 65 were invited to a concert and tea.

The newspapers referred to the school's history, *"The foundation stone was laid in 1874 and it opened with 107 scholars, then of all ages, about the same number as today.*

A low point in its fortunes was July 1938 when it closed because the register dropped to only 20 pupils. It re-opened during the early days of the 1939-45 war to accommodate London evacuee children and later catered for evacuees from Bristol.

The school was built for £1,129 excluding dues on stone quarried locally. Except for a cloakroom at the front and a slight adjustment at the rear, no enlargement or additions have been carried out during the 100 years.

At one time meals for 600 pupils of a number of schools in the area were cooked at Mount Hawke CP each day, supervised by Miss E I Vanstone of St Agnes.

The school now caters for junior children from Mount Hawke, Porthtowan and Mawla districts. A site has been bought for a new school adjoining the playing field opposite but no starting date has been set.

Miss Dawe's staff are Mrs Isabel Luff, deputy head, Miss D E Lloyd and Mrs J Greenslade with Mrs Thoroughgood part-time and Mrs June Lovering in charge of the four-year olds. Both Miss Dawe and Mrs Luff have taught there since 1946; when the school had only 36 pupils.

Members of the Mount Hawke Residents Association have presented two books for the school library to mark the centenary.

Lessons at the commemoration service, to be conducted by the Revd P D Williams, are to be read by 85 year-old Mr J E Tredinnick of St Agnes, one of the oldest surviving former pupils, and by a present-day Cornish-born scholar, Jack O'Shea of Porthtowan."

Robert Philby took over as head teacher on the 1st September 1975 and was to oversee an important event in the history of the school, the move to a new building.

On the 2nd April 1980 Mrs Mansell retired from helping with the school dinners. Not a momentous event in the life of the school but a moment's reflection on the name may indicate why it is included. At this time the number on the roll had increased to 137 and three years later this had gone up again…to 149.

The logbook entry for the 4th September 1986 states, "Vacated old school." A statement that does not adequately describe the tremendous amount of preparation and work involved in transferring all the trappings from a Victorian building to a modern school. The move, of course, was but a short distance but there must have been mixed emotions amongst the children and staff, not to mention past pupils. The old building may have been draughty and difficult to heat, it may not have compared favourably with the shiny new edifice, but it was familiar and held the memories of generations of schoolchildren.

But school life continued, at the new school in Roddas Road or, as some would still say, in Back Lane.

Ted Skimins was school caretaker for 25 years; he commenced in 1964 and was the last to hold the post in the old building and the first in the new.

Marlene Ball was already a voluntary helper at the school when Josephine Forway decided to resign her role of collecting the Porthtowan children from their bus at Penty-Bryn at 8.00am each day and taking them to school; Marlene applied for the job. In 1974 she began an involvement which was to last 25 years and include a variety of roles.

Pam Hayter was the school secretary at that time but in 1984 she was involved in an accident and Marlene was asked to stand in for her. Pam decided not to return to work and Marlene was successful in being appointed to the role which she held for 15 years. She attended 21 school camps and was involved in the Packathong fund-raising event, when many people from the village placed leaflets in packages for a national company.

Josie Greenslade of St Agnes retired in 1989; she recalled a couple of stories from her teaching days. *"I noticed a smell and gently enquired where it was coming from. I asked each in turn, 'Was it you John? Was it you David? Was it you Mary?' and so on. The response from each was a firm, ' No Miss.' Then one little boy looked up and said, 'Was it you Miss?'*

*One boy came up and said 'Please Miss, that Stephen ******* has been swearing and cursing,' I told him that I would deal with it. A little while later he came up again and said, 'Please Miss that bloody boy ******* has been swearing again.'"*

Disaster struck in late 1989 when the school was closed following a burglary. The thieves did considerable damage as they searched for items to steal but the total result of their efforts was just £35. As they made their way through the building they left a trail of damage out of all proportion to their ill-gotten gains. Doors were smashed, filing cabinets broken open and the contents strewn around. To give vent to their disappointment they even plastered the walls with food from the larder. Whether the perpetrators were caught or not we do not know but we like to think that they received some punishment for such a despicable crime.

In 1992 Mr Philby retired and deputy head Mrs Thoroughgood took charge pending the appointment of his replacement. Richard Burcher took over as head teacher on the 1st of January 1993; at that time there was 154 children at the school.

Maureen Townsend retired sometime around 2002; she had been working there since 1969.

The activities of a school are diverse and a dedicated team are required to deliver the curriculum set by the government; it is far removed from the days of the head teacher with one assistant.

The staff in 2008:

Head Teacher: Mr Richard G Burcher, Deputy Head Teacher: Miss Catherine Biddick, Class Reception: Mrs J Davidson, Class One: Miss R Goldsworthy, Class Two: Miss C Jouvenat, Class Three: Mrs C Powell, Class Four: Mrs J Williams / Mrs J Wood, Class Five: Mrs L Webb / Mrs L Cummins, Class Six: Miss C Biddick, SENCo: Mrs L Alcock, Teaching Assistants: Ms S Barker, Mrs C Brandreth, Miss B Collins, Mrs N Hopkins, Mrs P O'Keeffe & Mrs L Watson, Senior Lunchtime Supervisor: Mrs L Watson, Lunchtime Supervisors: Miss B Collins, Mrs S Green, Mrs J Hawkins & Mrs P O'Keeffe, Senior Secretary: Mrs N Hubbard, Receptionist/Telephonist: Mrs T Bassett, Cleaners: Ms D Pascoe & Mrs M Sell, Cook in Charge: Mrs S Pascoe, General Kitchen Assistant: Mrs L Spurrier.

Richard Burcher retired as head teacher in July 2008 and a surprise party of past and present pupils marked the occasion. Gordon Walker was appointed to the role for two terms while a permanent replacement is found.

The School continues to thrive and we are left to wonder what the teachers and pupils of the early years would make of the opportunities now available.

Organisations & Events

Whatever may change across the years there is one constant factor that links the generations…the flow of volunteers to organise the village events. Before the wealth of alternative entertainment the simple pleasure of such local events attracted huge crowds and the various clubs had no problem with numbers. It is more of a struggle now but many still thrive, they are the life-blood of any village.

Cottage Gardening Society: The first annual show was held in the third week of August 1919, the year after The Great War ended. The society offered its members the chance to attend demonstrations and exhibitions and to participate in the co-operative purchase of seeds, plants, and manures. Subscription was set at one shilling per year but ten-shillings and sixpence per year bought a Vice-Presidency.

Captain J Eslick was the first President, he was supported by two Vice Presidents, J Hichens and S Rodda. The committee comprised the Revd J H Beecroft, the Chairman, H O Bennetts, A Blight, R F B Harris, Ed Jeffrey, H Jose, J Pearce, E Rodda, G Tallack, E J Oats (Treasurer) and S O Bennetts (the hard working Secretary).

Lady Molesworth St Aubyn performed the opening ceremony for the second show, in August 1920, and commented that the dairy section was the finest in Cornwall.

Sports were held in the afternoon and there is a smattering of local names among the winners. There were flat races, obstacle races, pillow fights (won by J Bennetts), egg and spoon races, a boot race (whatever that is), thread the needle competition, high jump, apple race and cock fight. Norman Thomas won the silver medal for the highest number of points on the sports field. (RCG 18/8/20)

By 1923 ladies were serving on the committee; M Jones, C Mitchell, E M Pearce and S Tonkin were sharing the workload. The fifth Exhibition was held at Mount Hawke Council School on the 16th August.

In 1924 Phil Jones the cobbler won the President's Cup plus numerous other awards and Illogan Military Band were there to entertain.

In 1931 the Mayor of Truro, W H Cornew, opened the thirteenth annual event and praised the village for maintaining its independence and producing an excellent show. Mr John Kinsman, a former Chairman of the London Cornish Association, proposed a vote of thanks.

At the sixteenth show in 1934 the membership stood at almost 130 and the entries topped 620, a splendid effort for a village show. A wrestling tournament rounded off the day, the first in St Agnes Parish for 70 or 80 years. Mr W Tregoning Hooper of Falmouth organised it, he was the Secretary of the Cornwall County Wrestling Association. J H Triggs of Pool was the matcher and S Ham of Camborne, W Dunstan of Lanner and J Beard of St Day were the sticklers. First prize went to E J Lawry of Budock. (RCG 15/8/34)

Len Harvey, the famous boxer, was enlisted to open the show in one year; he was born at Stoke Climsland and held many titles.

In 1936 the entries were over 700; they were said to be of a high standard. R Blitchford won the most points for his paintings and W Butson was top for the best female bird. The day was concluded with a maypole dance performed by the school children. (RCG 19/8/36)

There were a huge number of classes in 1937; the show had been expanded to include Health Exhibits and a Utility Poultry Class. S Gilbert of Blackwater was Chairman, J M Butson of Goonown its Treasurer and the Secretarial duties were shared between Mr and Mrs H J Pearce of Ilfra House, Mount Hawke. From the names in the extensive list of committee members it seems that the Society had grown to include areas outside the village.

Many distinguished and well-known people were associated with the Society over the years; Lieut-Commander P G Agnew MP as President in 1937 and among its Vice-Presidents were Dr C Whitworth, J Kinsman and J Trounce.

Mary George recalled the evening activities which included tug of war, sheaf pitching, dog racing and cycle grass-tracking, all held in Mr Garland's field behind *Henly House.*

It would be interesting to know how long the Society continued and whether it ceased to exist or evolved into an organisation with a different name. I'm sure that someone will tell us, either before or after publication.

Art Classes: The village can hardly claim to be an art colony but it does seem that a number of artists have enjoyed its surroundings: Enreight Mooney during the early part of the 20th century, Geddes Cruickshank, Tony Giles, Ron Wood, John Hilton and perhaps others. John Hilton has exhibited his work in a number of locations including at The National Trust Gallery at Trelissick. During the late 1970s he ran a series of painting and sculpture classes in the Women's Institute Hall and many people benefited from his tuition.

Brass Band: In 1901 the village could boast its own fife and drum band and there is a suggestion that it once had its own brass band. Whether or not that is the case we cannot be sure but we have to say that we have our doubts. There is however an undoubted connection with the world of brass band, through the villagers who have played in St Agnes Silver Band and the eminent musician and conductor Derek Greenwood who now lives in the village. Derek started his banding career at Earby Silver Band in his home county of Yorkshire and in 1965 joined the Grenadier Guards where he became solo euphonium and played at the 1966 Wembley World Cup Final. In the 1970s he moved to Cornwall, to conduct Camborne Town Band. In his long musical career he has been involved with many other bands but it was with Camborne that he achieved his greatest success as he led them on two occasions to fourth place in the National Championships at the Royal Albert Hall.

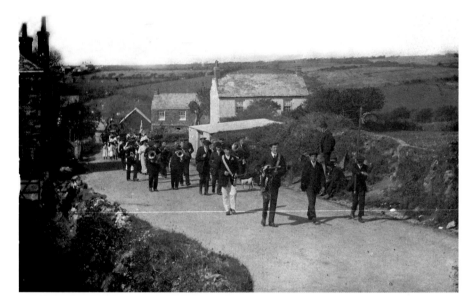

Possibly the Mount Hawke Brass Band participating in a village event (note the shed to the right from where Douglas Stephens sold his motor bikes)

Amateur Operatic Society: E M Hymes wrote an article in the 1977 Silver Jubilee Parish Programme. *"An Operatic Group produced a play annually which ran for three nights in the Council School, rehearsals being in the studio of Enright Mooney RA who lived at Chalcot. George Ward, the vicar's son, took part in some productions. He is now known as Michael Ward, actor, and sometimes appears on television."*

Mr H Pearce produced *Pearl the Fishmaiden* in 1931. M Rodda took the part of Lorenzo, the brigand chief and it seems that Miss D Parsons made a charming Pearl. Miss E Jones was Mistress Whelk and Mr A Climas, as Daddy Whelk, was the cause of much amusement. Other characters were played by K Bennetts, R Rodda, H Pearce, Miss J Carlyon, Miss F Tonkin and Miss B Harper and there were so many other names among the fish-maidens, brigands, floral dancers and mermaid dancers that it is a wonder that there were any villagers left to make up an audience. (RCG 18/3/31)

The Prince Royal Players: The group was formed in 1961 and were soon winning high praise for their productions. In 1966 they presented *Blithe Spirit* and Peter Wilkins recalled *Haul for the Shore*, he said, *"I played P C Widden and Nellie Pearce was also in it, she was a real scream."* Producer Betty Roberts resigned in 1975 and the group was disbanded.

Women's Institute Drama Group: The shows had been performed at the Women's Institute Hall and a number of members had been involved so it seemed natural that the organisation would step forward to fill the void. The group blossomed and began to form its own identity, taking the name of the **Penbron Players**. In 1978 it became independent as it separated itself from the mother organisation.

Carnivals: There is nothing quite like a village *do* to bring the community together, the common goal brings out the best in people but a lot of effort is required to get it just right. Carnivals require a tremendous amount of work and a number have been held over the years albeit not on a regular basis; the earliest recalled is in 1928.

An early carnival float...the names on the rear of the photograph are Cora Jones, Doris Jose & Dorothy Bennet

1948 – we think
Back row: Christine Foden, Jennifer Pascoe (now Martin) & Christine Harvey (we think).
Front row: Chris Chynoweth, Kit Wilkin & Roger Hocking.
It seems that there were to be two boy attendants but as three turned up for the judging they were all chosen. Wires must have been a little crossed however as Chris and Roger arrived in splendid blue whereas Kit turned up in pink.

Gala Days: Mount Hawke has a long history of village fairs or fetes but from 1968 to 1971 they were known as Gala Days. The events were organised jointly by the Mount Hawke Literacy Institute (Men's Institute) and the Women's Institute; six members from each formed the committee. Initially the venue was the Women's Institute Hall; Joe Pengelly and Tom Salmon from BBC Television are among the local celebrities who have performed the opening ceremonies.

A typical Gala Day began with a fancy dress parade headed by a brass band; the Fairy Queen and attendants, a large number of adults and the children followed this. In one year a *Pushball* competition was included; the ball was lent by the Avon Rubber Company and the competition sponsored by the Daily Express. There were plenty of other activities and stalls of every description. As ever, the refreshment tent was popular, on one occasion it dispensed eight gallons of ice cream, 490 cones, 200 pasties, 200 splits, 200 rolls and beefburgers, 200 saffron buns and a whole pile of fancy cakes. Ted Skimins held the purse strings and remembers the occasions as superb events with lots of fun.

1968 Gala Day winners
Back row: (L to R) Sharman Carlyon, Richard Stevens & Betty Tonkin.
Front row: Vivienne Stevens.

1969 Gala Day...Joy Forway was the Fairy Queen, Susan Hopley (left) and Juliet Townsend were her attendants, Manny Cockle is on the microphone and seated is Joe Pengelly.

1970 Gala Day...Crowds flock to enjoy the fun

Village Community Association: The Association was formed in 1974 and is still active. Chris Chynoweth said, *"With the arrival of the large housing developments in the village it was felt necessary to maintain the togetherness and community spirit of the village. Funds are used to support village activities and the committee responds to whatever is required. It may be outings or parties for the elderly or something for the young. It set up the Millennium Green and is a major contributor towards its maintenance but its major function is to organise the Village Day, a role it took over from the Gala Committee."*

After a break of eight years, a Village Fair was held at the Women's Institute Hall with some activities in the little field opposite. After several changes of venue it relocated to the extensive grounds of the new primary school. As the Women's Institute scrapbook said, *"It had become cramped in the little field but memory, tinged with nostalgia, turns cramped into cosy."* It was popular and gradually developed into a week of events.

In 1994 the weather was good and at the end of it the committee could look back with a good deal of satisfaction. On the Monday the Caddy family came out on top in the bicycle treasure hunt and the following day Scott Withecombe won the fun run and M A Belcher the seven-mile race. Wednesday was a more leisurely affair when Graham Bazeley examined local treasures in an Antiques Roadshow. The *Old School* Pub was the venue for a night of competition on the Thursday when teams showed off their skills with darts, skittles and general knowledge. Taking full advantage of home ground the Pub team took the honours.

These events were enjoyable enough but excitement was building for the Saturday Fair. Church Road was full of stalls and Helston Band led the parade through the village. Faye Webster was the Fairy Queen and Rebecca Simmons and Kate Doran the attendants. Daphne Skinnard of Radio Cornwall opened the event and judged the fancy dress which was won by Mount Hawke Playgroup with *Noah's Ark*. A disco rounded off the day and the week was concluded with a united service in the Methodist Chapel and a concert by Redruth Silver Band, Treverva Quartette and the inimitable Lilla Miller aka Mrs Rosewarne.

The first issue of Mount Hawke newsletter *In Touch* appeared in 1979. Chris and Hilary Chynoweth were on holiday when they read a local newsletter and felt that it was just what Mount Hawke needed. They floated the idea and it was accepted. It was choc full of events and notices and became an essential feature of village life. It was delivered free to the folk of Mount Hawke for about 27 years but in 2006 it was discontinued as an independent publication and incorporated into that excellent parish paper *The Bolster*.

1977… Sarah Hutton as the Silver Queen with attendants Jane Waters on the left and
Michelle Williamson

The **Millennium Green Trust** was set up in 2000 to develop and maintain
the large recreation area behind the chapel. This well used area is now an
impressive feature of the village.

The **Girls' Friendly Society** (Mount Hawke branch) was formed in 1926
with Mrs Ashley Rowe as President. On the 15th May 1928 twenty members were enrolled at a service conducted by the Chancellor, the Reverend
Canon Cooper; (Church logbook) numbers gradually rose to 32.

Dr W C Whitworth of St Agnes was enlisted to present a series of
lectures on first aid and as the group progressed Miss Playne designed a
branch banner which was made by Phyllis Tippett and Gwen Pheby. Joan
Chynoweth recalled the 1930s when Kathleen Rowe held the meetings at
her house near the railway halt. She said, *"We took part in drama productions
and competed against other societies. We even performed at the Royal Albert Hall."*

Rainbows is a lesser known organisation than Brownies and is directed
at girls in a younger age group. Hilary Chynoweth first began the First
Mount Hawke Rainbows in the mid 1990s; it had previously been based

in St Agnes. It currently has thirteen members who take part in a variety of activities on Tuesday afternoons in the Women's Institute Hall.

Brownies is an organisation for young girls aged between seven to ten and we believe that Mrs Williams of Porthtowan was the first Brown Owl. Hilary Chynoweth re-formed the unit in 1989 as the 1st Mount Hawke Brownies and ran it for about ten years. It met in the school and in 1994, in celebration of 80 years of Brownie Guiding, the unit buried a time capsule in the grounds there.

Girl Guides in Mount Hawke, (Wrens) commenced in 1935 or 1936 by Hilda Thomas and Miss Phyllis Benham who later married the Reverend Greaves. It made a successful start but it seems that the outbreak of war in 1939 caused it to close. Mrs Greaves re-opened the group in 1947 as the Blue-tit and Jenny Wren patrols; she was still running it in the 1950s; Mrs Bailey was also involved.

Chris Chynoweth was surprised that there were enough girls to start a group as according to his sister there were not many girls in the village at that time. He quickly added, *"Not that I had anything to do with them."* It seems that the third patrol (Bullfinches) was another group in later years.

Skatepark: Mount Hawke Youth Group was formed in 1982 to meet the needs of young people living in the immediate and surrounding rural communities. It met once a week in a hall for a few years but in 1988, following complaints about the noise and danger of street skateboards, an application was submitted to Carrick District Council for a dedicated skateboard park on wasteland near the village. Approval was granted on the basis of local need with the proviso that the facilities should be well organised. An application to Children in Need for funds proved successful and the Mount Hawke Youth Group (SK8) Park Project was awarded over £45,000.

An article by Pete Bramwell in the *West Briton* in September 2008 says that what began as a skate park has grown into a large operation; it is now a learning centre for youth development with courses on music, photography and multi-media.

Although quite close to the village it is possible that many people will not have visited the centre or appreciate what is on offer.

The interior of the Skatepark

Youth Clubs: There seems to have been more than one youth club or perhaps it was the same one that ran at different times. There was certainly one in the 1950s at the chapel, run by Jack Burrows, Monty's father. Apparently there were a few mishaps with the lights, maybe a bit of mischief, but the end result was its closure.

Cricket Club: Donald George recalled the cricket team both before and after the Second World War. *"During the 1930s the pitch was on halt road, at Penhallow Farm, but after the War it moved to Jack Rowe's field, on the right heading towards Menagissey."*

Mary George was quick to add, *"There was a girl's team as well."*

For a while matches were played behind the Victory Inn until the club re-located to it's own location … at the junction of Banns and the Towan Cross road.

In 1982 Mount Hawke and Porthtowan Cricket Club were playing in the Junior Division V and recorded what is referred top as a revenge win over Perranporth with a team comprised of S Ritchie, C Clay, S Grenfell, G Kent, M Pheby (Captain), C Pinches, T Major, N Greenslade, P Dower, R McCusker and C Looker.

The 1983 season in Junior League (Division 1V West) saw them complete their programme with a 100 per cent record … 18 wins from 18 matches.

The team photograph in a June 1984 newspaper comprised M Williams, N Greenslade, T Major, A MacDougall, C Pinches, S Nicholson, D Martin, M Pheby (Captain), C Looker, R McCusker, P Dower and the mascot, Strider the dog.

Football Club: Information is a bit sketchy but a club existed during the 1940s and was said to be for the youth of Mount Hawke, Towan Cross and Porthtowan. It aimed to promote a good sporting spirit, to maintain two soccer teams and to participate in matches for the Junior Cup (Mining Division) and the Dunn Cup. They played in Hartley Stevens' field in Halt Road; he was a brother of Garfield Stevens, their very able secretary.

Mount Hawke Football Team … 1947 or 1948
Back row (L to R): Garfield Hicks, Donald George, Ronnie Martin, Garfield Stevens & Morris Williams.
Middle row: Bobby Barkle, Clifford Hocking, Archie Pheby & Russell Pearce.
Front row: Bert Wherry & Brian Swallow.

The Gun Club was formed in 1971 by Roy Scoble, Roy May, Hugh Burley, George Dickinson and Mike Pheby; they shot clays with 12-bores on their site at Mingoose where they still meet. (Mike Pheby)

Tennis Club: The club began in the 1930s in a field at the top end of Rodda's Road. Joan Chynoweth recalled that her mother produced a number of concerts in the school to raise funds for it. According to Donald George the court was enclosed with corrugated galvanised sheeting fixed to railway sleepers. There was also netting at high level to avoid the loss of balls by the wayward hitters.

Internal championships were held each year and at the 1934 Whit Monday tournament A Pheby was victorious in the men's singles; the mixed title went to Miss Q Rowe and M Rodda.

Regular matches were arranged with other clubs and in 1933, against Chacewater, Miss F Gill, Miss E Rodda, Miss P Pheby, A Pheby, K Bennett and R Tatum produced a win for Mount Hawke. (St Austell Gazette 28/6/33) In July 1935 the home team lost to Truro St Mary's and Trehaverne but recorded wins over Redruth and St Stithians. There was no shortage of players; the list included Miss E Rodda, A Clynes (or Clymas), Miss P Pheby, A Pheby, Miss I Carlyon, P Hynes, K Bennetts and M Rodda. (RCG 17/7/1935)

The Literary Institute (Men's Institute) was formed in 1886 under the presidency of the Reverend John Dungey who presented a series of talks in a cottage near the post office. These were so popular that a larger room had to be found or built. Plans for a new building were put in place, Viscount Falmouth gave a piece of land and the members set about building their own premises.

John Passmore Edwards was a life-long champion of the working classes, a generous benefactor who provided funding for 70 public buildings throughout the country. Many were in Cornwall including the Institute in Blackwater, the village of his birth. It seems that Mount Hawke did not need his help with the building but was delighted to receive enough books to set up a reference library.

The *West Briton* of the 14th March 1988 referred to the erection of the new Miner's and Mechanic's Literary Institute which was said to be progressing favourably. It was to be single storey and consist of two rooms, one for literary purposes and the other for games. Even at that early stage the possibility of installing a billiard table was being considered.

The original concept of providing literary institutes was of a particular time…when opportunities for the improvement of the mind were few. As education improved and newspapers became more available the institutes evolved and eventually became best known for billiards and snooker.

Mr G J Smith of Truro opened the new Literary Institute in May 1889. In his speech he said that he hoped it would not degenerate into a mere club but that recreation would find a place there. He interpreted this as a change of labour of the mind from one subject to the other. To a man who had been toiling hard at bodily labour all day he recommended the Institute for the recreation of his mind. He considered that elementary education had opened the door and presented the golden key of knowledge to all the rising youth and he was sure that they were prepared to enter into the advantages of such an institute. (RCG 16/5/1889)

Local boy John Kinsman later wrote, *"Facing the chapel is our Institute… another example of voluntary work which speaks volumes for the character of our people. We started many years ago in a cottage; then we received a gift of land and set to work to erect a suitable building. In the valley is a quarry, the owner of which readily told us we could have the necessary stone free of charge. Our miners, in their spare time, raised the stone, our farmers carted it to the spot, numerous volunteers acted as labourers and the building was finished at a cost which seemed ridiculously small.*

For well over a quarter of a century it has ministered to the needs of the villagers, an example of self-help and enterprise which is not uncommon in the remoter parts of the Duchy. In the days when the only daily newspapers in the districts were those received by the parson and the schoolmaster, this Institute meant a great deal and many of those of whom we are proud got their first taste for literature within its walls. One of the early librarians loved good books so much that he thought it criminal to damage one of the volumes and many of his pupils have looked back with something akin to reverence at the passion he displayed for the masterpieces of literature."

Kelly's Directory of 1893 lists Rendle Langford as Secretary of the infant organisation and in 1897 it was F Langford (perhaps a relation or even the same person); in 1902 it was E Richards, perhaps the head teacher.

The *Royal Cornwall Gazette* of the 25th of February 1909 reported on a high tea held to raise funds. Mr Hitchens JP presided over a large gathering and after the tea the Tuckingmill Quartette gave a concert in the Council School.

W Jose was Secretary in the early 1900s but by 1914 if was F R Langford…perhaps, again.

Joan Chynoweth recalled, *"I think my mother must have often wondered what had happened to me when I was late home from school but there was always interesting things to see on the way. Next to the school was the Men's*

Institute and on fine days the door would be open and you could watch the men playing billiards. Across the road was Cowling's bakery and the lovely smell of baking bread. If I had to collect pasties for lunch I would see Mr and Mrs Cowling kneading dough and taking bread out of the oven. My father's workshop was around the corner and a few steps beyond that was Edgar Rodda's blacksmith's shop."

This 1925 photograph shows the Literary Institute in the centre with the school to the right and the Wesleyan Chapel in the distance

H Harper was the Secretary in 1930; by 1935 it was Montague (Monty) Rodda and in 1939, Herbert George Kalber. Claude Tonkin recalled the Institute when he was a young boy, in the 1930s. He said, *"You had to keep very quiet or you were out. I can remember some of the members at that time, there was Ashley Rowe, Bertie Thomas and George Tallack who was blind; he couldn't play snooker, of course, he would just go in for a chat."*

Dennis Barbary tried to join in the 1940s but was told by Mr Epplett that outsiders were not welcome. *"Fair enough,"* he said, *"I did come from Manor Parsley."* Will Carlyon soon put matters right and told Dennis' father that if he wanted to join then he was very welcome.

The 1950 Women's Institute scrapbook referred to the billiard team as the Champions of Cornwall; it also mentioned the recent extension to the building. The Carlyon family gave the land for this but some years later, when Graham Carlyon was a member of the committee, it was discovered that it had never been formally conveyed … the Institute had built on land it did not own. Graham quickly arranged for the formal conveyance and all was well.

Monty Rodda was Chairman and considered to be the best billiard player for miles. Shirley Barrett said that on a cold night Monty would send someone up to his home to collect some coal and wood for the Institute fire but Phyllis would tell them to burn their own. Apparently they used to pick it up anyway and run like hell.

The billiard team circa 1960
Back row (L to R): Claude Lockett, C Delbridge & Archie Pheby.
Front row: Francis Garland, Monty Rodda (Captain) & George Langford.

During the 1960s support for the Institute was not good and it closed for four or five years. The building was boarded up but it was regularly vandalised and became an unsightly mess. Somehow the snooker table survived and following a show of support it re-opened and the click of cue on ball was heard again.

We live in an ever-changing world and a glance around the parish suggests that the snooker table will go the way of the reading room. It seems that with so many other attractions, institutes are no longer popular and the struggle to maintain them falls on few shoulders. But whatever the future may hold there is no doubt that Mount Hawke Literary Institute fulfilled its original objective.

Old Cornwall Society: The *Royal Cornwall Gazette* carried the headline, *"Another Old Cornwall Society."* At its first meeting, in the church hall, Mr C D P Roberts was elected Chairman of the new Society which had 120 members. Miss J Tremain of St Agnes, the St Agnes Pantomime Ballet Dancers under Mrs Hayward and the Mount Hawke String Orchestra provided the entertainment.

The Society was formed in 1950 and promised to adhere to the principles set down by the founder members of the first society, in St Ives, *Gather ye the fragments that are left, that nothing be lost.*

The new committee began arranging events: lectures, concerts, art exhibitions and during the summer months, tours of places of interest across Cornwall.

Gladys Johns (later Thomas), an early Treasurer, recalled that most of the indoor activities were held in the church hall with committee meetings at the home of the President, at *Phylmont,* opposite *Henly House.*

It had undoubtedly started with a flourish but it quickly hit rough waters and with no one willing to take over as President the Society was suspended ... the last official meeting was held on the 30th November 1960.

Happily there was a phoenix from the ashes and in March 1964 St Agnes Old Cornwall Society was formed, or more correctly re-formed*; among the new members were some who had been involved at Mount Hawke. According to Frank Carpenter in *A Millennium Chronicle,* money held by the trustees of the Mount Hawke Old Cornwall Society was transferred to the newly formed Society. He said, *"This then saw the final closing of the Mount Hawke Old Cornwall Society."*

(* Based on evidence uncovered by Peter [Nick] Thomas who found that there were two Old Cornwall Societies in St Agnes prior to the present one. A 1926 issue of the Old Cornwall Journal lists W H Gribbin of Goonown as the Honorary Secretary but a 1932 issue states that Wilfred Sarre of Trevellas was acting as Local Recorder at St Agnes because there was no Society there; the one which existed in 1926 had clearly ceased by then. In 1933, the journal states that the St Agnes Preservation Society had recently formed an Old Cornwall Society at St Agnes but this in turn ceased to operate and the present one, the third, was set up in 1964.)

Women's Institute: The movement was formed in 1915 with two clear aims: to revitalise rural communities and to encourage women to become more involved in producing food during the First World War. Since then its aims have broadened and it is now the largest women's organisation in the United Kingdom with over 200,000 members in its 6,800 branches.

On the 2nd December 1946 a meeting was held in Mount Hawke Primary School to consider the possibility of starting a Women's Institute in the village. Twenty-nine people attended and following an address by Mrs Flamank, the Voluntary County Organiser, Mrs Harper proposed and Mrs Pearce seconded that an Institute be formed. It was carried unanimously and all those present joined. Nominations were received for a committee and a Foundation Meeting was held on Monday 9th December 1946 when the first officers and committee were elected.

President	Mrs F Harper.
Vice Presidents	Mrs M Mitchell and Mrs N Pearce.
Hon. Secretary	Mrs M Vincent
Hon. Treasurer	Mrs N Maclaine
Committee	Mrs Barnet, Mrs Chynoweth, Mrs Jose, Miss G Rodda, Miss Rogers, Mrs Rowe and Mrs Thomas.

The initial committee meeting was held at the President's home and the first full meeting, in January, in the church hall. The subscription was set at half-a crown (12.5p); one shilling for Affiliation Fee (five pence to National Federation and seven pence to the County Federation) and one shilling-and-six-pence for branch funds.

The Vicar, the Revd Greaves, offered the hall for meetings and always ensured that the room was welcoming with the lights turned on and the fire lit. Unfortunately the open fire was a problem, it smoked so much that most winter meetings were accompanied by fits of coughing.

A choir was formed in March 1947 with Miss G Rodda as conductor and Mrs Carter as accompanist. Membership increased quickly and in June the Institute entered its first competition, at the Royal Cornwall Show. The following month the members produced their first stage performance, in the church hall. Later that year Mrs Carlyon was placed second in the Hanson Cup competition and Mrs Harper travelled to London as the delegate at the national meeting in the Royal Albert Hall. Mrs Thomas and Mrs N Pearce organised a National Savings Group and a teapot, jugs, nine dozen cups, saucers and plates were bought from Docking's shop in St Agnes.

The first birthday party, in December, must have been quite an occasion. It was held in the church hall where the kettle had to be boiled on the open fire, the smoky open fire. This resulted in smoke-flavoured tea and tea-makers blackened by smuts. Shortly after, an electric boiler was installed.

Enthusiasm was high as the new club formed a drama group and prepared for its first production, *A Christmas Carol*. Phyllis Greaves was Ebenezer Scrooge, Margaret Vincent became Bob Cratchet and Nellie Pearce was Mrs Cratchet. But who would play little Tiny Tim? Making his stage debut in this starring role was none other than four year-old Monty Burrows.

The Annual Outing was a feature of the early years, before car ownership was so widespread. The first, in June 1948, was to Cheddar Gorge in a Carter Bros coach. Others followed, to Bournemouth (organised by Nellie Pearce and described by Christine Pearce as a marathon), Bath, Weymouth, Longleat and Cardiff (when the coach driver lost his way) but one deserves special mention, the 1954 trip to the Channel Islands…a day trip! The coach left Mount Hawke at 4.45am and the party of 20 travelled via Torquay to Guernsey for four and a half hours of sightseeing and shopping. The hardy bunch were back in the village at 2.30am and after a few hours rest Mrs Green was out delivering milk, Mrs Pearce was sorting the letters and the two male *chaperons* were out on their farms.

1949…The Choir in Truro City Hall
Back row: Mrs West, Mrs Williams, Miss Hoadley, Mrs Rogers, Mrs Hoskins, Mrs Carter & Mrs Frost.
Centre row: Mrs Snell, Miss M Green, Mrs Rodda, Mrs Pearce & Mrs Bennetts.
Front row: Miss M Cocking, Mrs Chynoweth, Mrs Green, Mrs Blackmore & Mrs O Thomas.

A piano was soon purchased and Mrs Vincent's keep fit classes were underway. Food rationing was still in place and each member was required to arrive at meetings with her teaspoonful of tea. In 1950 it was the year of the village scrapbook, a portrait of local history and life; what a contribution to social history it became.

Cigarette smoke was causing a problem and the ladies were asked to refrain from lighting up during business meetings.

1950…Old English Fair
Back row: Nellie Pearce, Mrs Frost, Mrs Garland, Mollie Walters, Mrs Tippett, Valetta Maud Roach, Olga Thomas and Mrs Chynoweth.
Centre row: Mrs MacClean, Mrs Heppenstall, Mrs Green, Mrs Blackmore, Philadelphia Snell and Gladys Simmons.
Front row: Sylvia Carlyon, Edna Rowe, Mrs Booth, Prudie Bennetts and Miss Audrey Gribben.

The BBC programme *Any Questions* was popular in 1952 and John King of Mithian was enlisted as question-master for a local production. Miss Jones (Welfare Officer), Miss Dawe (Headmistress of Mount Hawke Primary School), Dr Henry Whitworth and Mr Godber (Nursery Gardener, Perranporth) formed the Mount Hawke panel.

In February the Members joined with the entire country to show their respect as they stood in silence for the late King George VI.

Although the Branch was only a few years old the talk was of buying some land for a permanent home of their own. An enquiry was made about a plot owned by Mrs Richards and an offer of £75 submitted, subject to planning approval. Mr George had been renting the land and he confirmed that he was willing to relinquish his tenancy.

The Planning application was successful, the site purchased and trustees appointed: Mrs G Simmons, Mrs M Mitchell, Mrs O Thomas, Mrs W Green and Mrs M Sampson. Mr George was then asked if he would sell a small parcel of land adjacent to the site but he kindly gave it and a small shed was erected for equipment.

Having purchased the site the members now looked around for a suitable building and a group set out for Ugbrooke, Kingsteignton, to inspect a 20 feet by 40 feet hut previously used by American soldiers during the Second World War. It was considered suitable and purchased for £75.

Mr Stephens and the members' husbands erected the building, eighty-five folding chairs were purchased at a cost of ten shillings each and in May 1953, Mrs Treloar of St Agnes performed the opening ceremony.

The new Women's Institute Hall

The opening ceremony

The next Harvest Festival was held in new hall, the proceeds going to Cheshire Homes. Grists of Plymouth presented a film show which included the Coronation and members were delighted to win the cup at the Camborne Fat Stock Show.

In January 1954 the members stood in silence as a tribute to Mrs Harper, their first President.

Around this time electricity was installed, a new porch was added, stage rails and curtains put up and new entrance gates set in place.

1955...The Dutch Evening
Back row (L to R): G Simmons, Mrs Harvey, Mrs Snell, Mrs Mewton, Mrs M Sampson, Mrs Chynoweth, H Murrish, Miss West & Miss Rogers (one name missing).
Middle row: Mrs Pearce, Mrs Carlyon, Mrs Mannell, Mrs Green, Mrs O Thomas, Mrs N Maclaine & Mrs Dexter.
Front row: Mrs I Williams, Margaret Hicks, Margaret Green & May Hocking (one name missing).
And...yes, you've guessed it, little Graham Carlyon.

The 19th birthday celebrations in 1965 also marked the Golden Jubilee of the National Federation and a party was organised to mark the two events. Mrs Pearce, a founder member and one of the first Vice-Presidents, received a presentation; it also marked her retirement as village postmistress, after 24 years.

The 1965 celebration dinner
Top table (L to R): E Hynes, O Thomas, D Liddicoat, (County Chairman), I Carter, E Donnelly
(County Treasurer), G Simmons, P Andrews (County Secretary) & W Green.
Side table: S Crossland, Mrs Wilkins, Miss Bennett & Mrs Maclaine.
Long table (clockwise): Mrs Wilson, Mrs Butler, Mrs Dunstan, Miss V Richards, Mrs Walters,
Mrs Dexter, Mrs Snell, Miss G Rodda, Mrs S Pearce, Miss Goyne, Miss M Rodda, Mrs Williams,
Mrs Trengove, Mrs Mulaby, Mrs Woodbridge & Mrs MacPherson.

Mrs Thomas attended a Royal Garden Party at Buckingham Palace in 1966 and in 1967 a field day in Natural History was held at Chapel Porth when a study was made of forms of life found in a large cave, the last study before the Torrey Canyon disaster devastated the area.

The Silver Birthday Celebration 14th December 1971 with Maureen Townsend, Olga Thomas, E Hynes & E Sprague

By 1978 the building was beginning to show its age and the roof was replaced and some windows repaired. A year later saw the production of another scrapbook with the title *The Changing Farm 1900 to 1980*.

In 1980 the Women's Institute produced a competition piece entitled *The History and Natural History of our Local Footpaths*. It contained some interesting guide maps and many snippets of information about the area. It described Tywarnhayle stream, which begins in the village where it enters the Little Wood, and runs through Park Shady which, it suggests, properly refers only to the wooded part of the stream's course rather than the whole valley. At the far end of the valley, where the Tywarnhayle water runs under the road and enters the Porthtowan Stream, another path runs back up the valley to skirt the tree's around Mouse's Well and join Croft Prince Lane.

Another route was through Old Church Lane and Penhaul Lane (now Penhallow Way) and over Blind Tippett's to where it fans out into three, more or less, parallel tracks. Two of these lead to *Penhallow Farm* and the third to swampy ground.

Blind Tippett's Well was capped when Trenithick Estate was built. Chris Chynoweth suggests that this could have been an airshaft, rather than a well, for the Gover Adit of the Great St Vincent Mine, the portal of which is by the old millpond.

The following was written in January 1982 as the epilogue to the Story of the Women's Institute.

"The preparation of this history story has enabled us to ponder the development of our institute over the past 35 years.

The social changes in our village are probably shared with all other rural communities in this country; fewer and larger farms, fewer farm workers, more mothers in employment outside the home, more unemployed and, probably, an increase in the average age of the community. As this is being written we learn that a neighbouring Women's Institute fears it may have to close because of declining membership; sad news indeed. It would seem that we are in an era when the Women's Institute meeting has to compete against the pull of a cosy evening at home by the television. The young woman who goes out to work cannot be chided for spending her evenings with her family. The elderly woman may be loath to walk to the meeting through an unlit village street. But our members are good and, with an active membership, Mount Hawke Women's Institute should continue to evolve and flourish."

In July 1996 Mount Hawke Women's Institute celebrated its 50th anniversary. It enjoyed the company of three founder members: Caroline Wilkins, Mary Rodda and Mrs Reynolds (née Kinsman). The official Birthday Dinner in the December was a grand affair with the hall decked out like a restaurant and a sumptuous meal prepared by Leslie and Robert Jones.

In 2008 Mary Rodda reflected, *"The organisation recently celebrated its 60th anniversary and now I'm the only founder member still alive."*

There have been many other clubs and organisations in Mount Hawke over the years and, of course, some still exist.

The Trenithick Residents' Association is based on the housing development by Cumber Homes. The Keep Fit Club, Hockey Club and Old Time Dancing Group, Whist Drives (running since the 1960s and still going strong), Gardeners' Club, Craft Quilters (busy in the Women's' Institute Hall on Thursday evenings) and the Diet Club (performing miracles, or not, in the cause of shedding the Christmas and Easter excess) provided plenty of variety for the adults.

For the young there is, or was, the Pre-School Groups and Play Group and going back a few years, the Boy's Brigade. For the seniors; The Friendship Club and Age Concern.

The West of England Steam Engine rally is not a Mount Hawke event but it does take place on a site near the village, in fact for one or two years it was even closer… in a field between the halt and the village.

There were other village activities that were not associated with just one, or even any, organisation. The impromptu events like the firework display. Ted Skimins said, *"I used to go around the village with the kids on my trailer, collecting material for the fire which we built in Carlyon's field. People gave us fireworks or money."*

There was even a comic football match, arranged and refereed by Neddie Mewton. It seems that he carried a hip flask to revive the wounded. It was filled with whisky and by the end of the match the players were queuing up to be injured.

The comic football match in the 1950s

As we sat in Ted Skimins' front room, the very spot where Jack Cowling's bakery once stood, a picture began to build of a village intent on enjoying itself. This must be apparent from the long list of organisations, a list which is probably incomplete. We apologise for any omissions.

Stories & Reminiscences

Just like every community Mount Hawke has its characters, the prim and the proper, the zany and the slightly eccentric. It has its stories too, both amusing and sad and we hope that this short collection gives a flavour of life across the years. We have included those that we found most interesting and, of course, that were decent enough for a book of this type. If you cannot find yours then we will not be drawn on the reason for its exclusion, perhaps it was simply because of the lack of space.

Tywarnhayle Mine Count House was built in the early 1800s, near the eastern entrance of the valley that leads to Park Shady. It was the administrative centre for the mine, where the miners collected their pay. There are other buildings in the vicinity and during a refurbishment in the 1820s, a shoe (possibly a horse-shoe) was found built into a chimneybreast. Apparently the old miners considered that this provided good luck; it was replaced and is presumably still there.

Circa 1930s... A view of Wheal Music (Navvy Pit) to the right and the lane on the left snaking its way up the valley towards Park Shady

In April 1827 Joseph Gribin was returning from a funeral at St Agnes; he was walking some way behind his companions. As he rushed to catch up with them two men attacked him, near Gover. They jumped over a hedge and struck him with a stick. One of them stole a £1 note from his pocket and the other threatened him with a pistol. They grabbed his watch and Gribin said, *"I know the number on it."*

One of the men shouted, *"Kill him,"* a shot was fired but it missed.

At that Gribin called out, *"Murder!"* and the men ran off. The next morning the watch was found but without the chains or seals. Gribin said, *"It made it too dangerous for them to hold it or attempt to sell or pawn it."* (West Briton)

Mount Hawke suffered greatly during the cholera epidemic in the 1830s with nine deaths within a fortnight. Even the local doctor was laid low and help was difficult to find. (RCG 30th Nov 1833) Charles Doble, a surgeon, was appointed to the role of doctor for the duration of the crisis and was generous in his praise of The Reverend W H Snowe, the curate of St Agnes, who, he said, had acted with great courage in visiting the homes of the sick and dying. *"He was the means of inspiring me with greater confidence in the performance of my duties."*

On the 7th October 1842 four-year old Mary Jane Whitford was alone in the cottage; her father was at work and her mother outside milking a cow. There was an open hearth and the assumption is that she leant across it to reach something on the mantle. Her clothes caught alight and she was so severely burned that she only survived a few hours.

Ashley Rowe wrote that kitchen ranges were very few and became a cherished possession. At the Great Exhibition of 1851, John Argall of St Agnes showed his model of an improved Kitchen Apparatus. This was described as being adapted for baking, boiling and roasting with one fire. Mr Rowe wrote, *"It is possible that a kitchen apparatus made by John Argall may still be in use in the district. I have heard the Cornish Range referred to as 'the apparatus' by some of the older people of Mount Hawke. When one remembers the terrible dangers of the open hearth it is easy to understand the great pride which country folk took in the smart appearance of Cornish Ranges. Until quite recently these were regarded as tenants' fixtures and strangers from up-country, having obtained possession of a cottage in this district, often experienced a severe shock when they beheld a yawning gap in the kitchen wall, the previous occupiers having taken the stove to their new abode."*

A typical Cornish Range

Even though Mount Hawke was made a separate ecclesiastical parish in 1847, interments still took place at St Agnes, a journey of two miles or more.

Walking funerals were common with the coffin carried by relays of bearers.

In December 1851 the *West Briton* reported a lecture at the Truro Institution by Thomas Garfield, a well-known writer and lecturer. He referred to the animosity between the inhabitants of the north and south side of the parish. *"Although it might seem incredible... in the case of a funeral when the corpse was taken from the south side (Mount Hawke) to the churchyard in the north, it was considered dangerous for the bearers to go all the way to the Churchtown; and it was thought necessary to have a relay of men from the north part of the parish to meet the funeral about half a mile from the churchyard and bear the corpse there, otherwise there was almost a certainty that even the solemnity of a funeral would be interrupted by a fight."*

Ashley Rowe commented *"There was no contradiction of this story and I suppose, in view of Thomas Garfield's reputation, it must be accepted. Friction between adjacent villages was at one time very real; St Agnes and Mount Hawke were in no way exceptional in this but it is doubtful whether the animosity was actually carried to the lengths suggested by Thomas Garland."*

It seems that walking funerals were often held on Sundays because of the availability of sufficient bearers. In a 1958 article he described one particular occurrence. *"A Mount Hawke miner, now dead, told me that as a small boy he had been sent on a weekday to intercept miners coming off core at Wheal Charlotte because there were insufficient bearers for a funeral. The coffin would be carried by six men, the remaining bearers walking two by two behind it, followed by the singers and mourners. At a signal from the undertaker the coffin was halted and the foremost bearers would come up and take the place of those carrying it; the original bearers would stand at the sides of the road and then take their place at the end of the party. On a long journey this would be repeated many times."*

In May 1858 Charles Trebilcock, a six-year old boy, was knocked down and killed by a horse ridden by William Michell of the London Inn, Redruth. At the inquest the jury returned a verdict of accidental death but as Michell was said to be riding very fast he was asked to pay the family some compensation. It is a measure of the value placed on the lives of ordinary people that William Michell was not even required to attend the inquest.

One of the worst blizzards ever known in these parts occurred in March 1891. Trees were torn up, roofs blown off and the snow was several feet deep. At the funeral or Mrs Milford Wilkin's grandfather the bearers had to carry the coffin along the tops of the hedges as the roads were impassable. (W I book)

Blackwater Band was said to be one of the best in the district but this is not borne out be any contest results and may be considered a tad fanciful. It was engaged for Mount Hawke Band of Hope tea-treat and when the procession reached Short Cross it turned right towards Porthtowan. The band followed but the bass drummer, a rather short man who could not see over the top of his drum, went straight ahead, towards Menagissey.

To avoid a re-occurrence it is said that he decided to cut two windows through the drum so that he could see where he was going and, of course, where the rest of the band had gone. Blackwater people say that it wasn't his decision; he was told to have windows put in or resign from the band.

A lovely story, you can believe it if you will but it is one that seems to apply to just about every band in Cornwall.

Blackwater Reed & Brass Band at Mount Hawke tea-treat in what is now the Millennium Green

According to Ashley Rowe, John Kinsman was one of the earliest pupils of Mount Hawke School. He studied shorthand and made a successful career in London. He was an active member of the London Cornish Association and was credited with having convinced many Londoners that Mount Hawke was the capital of Cornwall.

We have included a number of items by John Kinsman whose book, *The Cornish Handbook*, was written in 1920. In its preface he wrote, *"When the conditions of modern life decreed that I should join the throng of Cornish people dwelling in the Metropolis, I discovered that the way to be happy in London was never to lose touch with the Land of Romance.*

Regular visits to the Delectable Duchy enabled me to continue those studies of Cornish characteristics which I had begun in the quietude of Mount Hawke; and, gradually, the vision of a handbook dealing with various aspects of Cornish life and history took form.

My own contributions are the result of much walking and cycling through secluded hamlets and villages; and the habit of spending glorious hours in the carpenters', the blacksmiths' and the bootmakers' workshops and in the mines, where, even now, rich veins of folk-lore are to be found."

Sir Arthur Quiller-Couch wrote an introductory chapter in which he said, *"In the remoter parts of Cornwall to this day a visitor or 'up-country' man is spoken of as 'the foreigner,' though he come from no more distant a land than the county of Devon; and I dare say that, in thought at any rate, he makes haste to return the compliment. He soon feels that 'the Duchy' is not a part of England, as he knows England."*

Edward James Nankivell was born not far from the school and, like John Kinsman, found employment in London. He studied shorthand from old notebooks found in a cupboard in a cottage adjacent to his father's carpenter's shop and later became the official shorthand writer in the Law Courts and the City Editor of the Pall Mall Gazette.

There were many old Cornish games and pastimes, now lost to memory. One was known as *Tips*, played by miners. It comprised two teams who passed a button from hand to hand under a table. We imagine that the purpose was to guess in whose hand it was. *Pitch and Toss* with halfpennies was a game particularly associated with Good Friday for some reason and *Quoits and Lampings* was a beach game, often played at Porthtowan. (W I book)

John Kinsman talked of Cornish dialect and of how he loved to sit and listen to the conversations in the local tradesman's shops. He said that he had heard this story while he was sitting quietly in the corner of the bootmaker's workshop in a village overlooking the cliffs at Porthtowan; it may be a little difficult to follow but it is worth persevering.

"That was a grand hymn up to praichen last night, Blaw ye the Trumpet, Blaw. It reminded me of the ould shawman who used to come 'round every winter and who slaiped in Maister Thomas's barn. You knaw, Jones, he got so used to slaipen there that he never thought of doin' anything but walking straight in and

lyin' down in the loft; and the next day he would give hes shaw and go through hes performance on the great ould trumpet he always played. Waun time, however, the roof of the chapel falled down and, while it was bein' mended, the mittins wor held in Maister Thomas's barn. The ould shawman arrived and dedn knaw nawthin' about this. He traapsed up to the farm, went into the barn without maakin' any more noise than a mouse, and went to slaip in the loft as sound as a cat. Soon afterwards, the people from the chapel traapsed in, for their mitten'; but maister shawman slaiped on. Then, the praicher gov out the hymn. Says he: 'We will sing together the ould familiar hymn – Blow ye the Trumpet, Blaw.'

He had a good voice and it waaked up the shawman and when the praicher gov out the naame agen, the ould man said to himself, 'Ah, somebody must have found out I'm here, but I wonder why they want me to play the trumpet.'

'Blaw ye the Trumpet, Blaw,' the praicher hollowed agen, and the ould man, thinkin' there was nawthin' else for it, picked up hes great brazen trumpet and blawed for all he was worth. Aw my dears, you shud have seen the people. They thought ould Nick himself was after them, and they tore out of the barn and down the road like hares. I never hear that hymn without thinkin' av it."

The *West Briton* of the 19th November 1896 included the story of a carnival but it left us wondering at the purpose of it all. *"On Friday night it was estimated that three hundred persons turned out at Mount Hawke to witness what was publicly announced in the village as 'A Carnival'. A procession was formed, preceded by a banner bearing the inscription, 'I will do right or restore fourhold.' Immediately following came a donkey, on which was mounted an effigy of a man, a band of young musicians and the hundreds of spectators brought up the rear. After the village was paraded, the effigy was tied to a stake, saturated with oil and set on fire amid the shouts of the on-lookers. The proceedings caused great excitement in the neighbourhood, as the circumstances which led up to them have been almost the sole topic of conversation for some weeks past."*

Standing in the churchyard at Mount Hawke is a memorial to the men of the *Rose of Devon*, lost on the treacherous cliffs at Porthtowan on Monday the 29th November 1897.

The sea had been running wild for some time and it was not surprising when wreckage was spotted. Shortly after, two bodies were washed up on the beach and four others were found in the rocks. Apart from their belts bearing the name *Rose of Devon*, none could be immediately identified. Before long the barque itself was spotted, stuck fast in the sand about two hundred yards below high water mark. Fragments of wreckage were strewn across the beach and soon collected by salvers. It was thought that the vessel was disabled a long way out and driven on to the beach.

Writing in the St Agnes Museum Trust Journal, Clive Benney states, *"Two (of the men) were wearing oilskin coats but the others had only ordinary working garments. The finest man is nearly six feet high, strongly built, with a lightish moustache and on his right wrist and hand a bracelet and anchor are tattooed… Next to him was a man of about sixty, of medium height, with beard and moustache turning grey. Then came a clean-shaven young man, about thirty, with delicate features and dark hair, he appeared to be the mate. By his side was one of the same age, with very dark brown moustache. Next was a young man with dark hair and a sixth was about thirty years old, with slight dark beard and moustache."*

Chief Coastguard Vines of Porthtowan took charge of the bodies and P C Benney of St Agnes (Clive Benney's great grandfather) reported the details to the coroner.

When the tide receded it was found that the vessel had broken in two, one half having been dashed to pieces, while the other was held fast in the sand by the bow, which pointed seaward.

The outhouse where the bodies were laid was said to be far from suitable. It was a miserable old shed with walls riddled with rat holes. The six bodies lay close together on the ground, no attempt had been made to remove the sand and blood from them.

At the inquest at Towan Cross the Revd J Stona of Mount Hawke was chosen as foreman of the jury. Witnesses confirmed that they had seen no lights or signals; there had been nothing to suggest that there was a vessel in distress.

The jury returned its verdict, *"Found drowned."*

Concern was expressed regarding the temporary resting place of the bodies and after discussion P C Benney asked if the coroner would recommend that the bodies be removed to the mortuary at St Agnes but added, *"They object to the four found in Illogan Parish being removed to that mortuary because of the expense to this parish."*

The Coroner replied that it was immaterial to him where they were taken as long as they were looked after. He instructed PC Benney to discuss it with the overseers of both parishes.

Coastguard West reported, *"We passed the place at intervals last night and gave the door a rap with a stick to frighten away the rats."*

The coroner thought the bodies might remain another day before being buried, for identification purposes. He thought that the owners of the vessel would bear the expenses of the funerals and he supposed that there would be no difficulty on that point.

It seems that it took a public outcry before the bodies were eventually buried. Instructions were given by two of the men's families, Loveridge and Machon, that they were not to be buried locally.

The memorial to the crew of the *Rose of Devon* in Mount Hawke graveyard

In 1899 John Thomas Blackney wrote his journal; it was timely as he died the following year. He was born in Mount Hawke on the 6th September 1828 and left Cornwall in 1852, to work in the mines of South America. After a short period back in this country, in 1858, he left for North America where his family joined him. He was a Cornishman who travelled far and lived an interesting life; the 5th Journal of the St Agnes Museum Trust includes his story, it is well worth reading.

Circa 1900 ... The post office and lane leading to Rope Walk ... note the old well in the centre

Frank Carpenter told the sad story of an event in 1901 when Mary Elizabeth Phillips, aged two and a half years, was found drowned in a water butt. Her mother was found guilty of her murder but declared to be insane.

In November 1906 a fire at Menagissey destroyed two houses and a barn near to some workings of Wheal Ellen Mine. Mrs Jeffrey had done her baking on the Friday but did not light the fire the following day. The assumption was that as the fire had started at that end of the building it must have been smouldering throughout the night. The thatched roof caught fire and soon the whole block was ablaze. As was often the case, the occupants took a considerable risk in saving the furniture. (RCG 15th November)

The cottages after the fire

The *Royal Cornwall Gazette* of the 27th of February 1908 carried a story of an accident which could have had a grim outcome. *"Mr Uren, merchant, had got into a trap, when somehow the bridle slipped off the horse's head and the animal bolted. It galloped through the village towards Navvy Pit where it turned in on some mine burrows. The trap was smashed but Mr Uren, who was flung out, escaped with severe shock and a few bruises. The horse also escaped without serious injury."*

A concert on the 26th October 1910 in aid of the Royal Cornwall Infirmary and the Miners' Hospital at Redruth was clearly a grand occasion. A committee of ladies and gentlemen of the village organised it and the school was crowded to hear a long and excellent programme chaired by Captain Eslick. The Mount Hawke String Orchestra played two selections and Miss Jennie Gulliver, Miss Ethel Channon, Miss Nellie Gulliver, Howard Kistler, Sidney Clark were the singers. Miss Salome, Miss Hilda Barfett and Miss Tilley performed a comedy entitled *The Suffragettes*. The total raised was £12.10s and the *Royal Cornwall Gazette* concluded with the comment, *"Excellent, Mount Hawke."*

Circa 1910…Drawing water from an old standpipe on the hill down to Banns…
(L to R): John Henry Parsons (on horseback), Tamsin Richards, Dorothy ?, Maude Jones with
children Cora & Will (Phil Jones' family) & unknown

On the 22nd June 1911 every town and hamlet paid loyal homage to King
George V as they celebrated his coronation. The morning drizzle cleared
at noon and the children's festivities took place in fine weather. (RCG
29/6/1911)

Will Jones referred to the practice of serenading newly married couples.
He said, *"When Sam Gribben was married we went down to his place and
banged tin pans until they brought out some food or whatever; we called them
kettle drums."* This seems to have been quite common and we have heard of
the musicians referred to as kitley bands but the name seems to vary across
Cornwall.

Mains water supply came to the village relatively early…in 1920 but according to Frank Carpenter some people elected to continue using the standpipes located around the village. It seems that any household within 200 feet
of a standpipe was deemed to have a supply and was subject to water rates.

About halfway between *Pollys* crossroads and *Little Coosewartha Farm*,
over the hedge on the left, is an old concrete reservoir, shown on the 1907
OS Map as Truro R D C Water Works. This was used to supply the various

standpipes around the village and Chris Chynoweth recalled that when it became redundant it was a popular play area for the youngsters.

According to the Women's Institute scrapbook, "*Water supply must have been one of the housewife's chief concerns; Miss Rodda remembers her mother saying that in dry weather she began collecting water on the Monday evening ready for the following Monday's wash. The family then lived in the village and, with the other villagers, had to go down to the 'Splash' near the water mill or to the stream at the foot of Gover Hill for their water. Mrs Mutton recollects 'Water Parade' on Saturday evenings when a hurried rush was made by all to get in water, none was supposed to be fetched or drawn on Sunday. The usual method of transport was in anker barrels, the name given to small wheelbarrows fitted with a barrel having a wooden cork. Some wells, worked by windlass, were in existence and one at the rear of the present post office can still be seen.*"

Every village has its tragedies and Mount Hawke has had its share. We are unsure of the exact dates but these four, recalled by Will Jones, were particularly poignant as they involved young people.

Edgar Rodda was gardening near his blacksmith shop and was using a two-clawed digger (a biddex) to lift potatoes. As he dug into the ground a young lad was picking them up. The boy was no doubt keen to help but in his eagerness he ventured too close and was struck on the head and killed.

Neddie Mewton was driving his traction engine up through the village when a young lad ran out into the road, straight in front of the vehicle. Perhaps Neddie didn't see him or maybe he couldn't stop in time but the boy was crushed to death under one of the huge wheels.

Will Jones and some friends had just come out of the sea at Porthtowan when one of them decided to have one more swim. Will said, "*We waited for him but he suddenly disappeared. We tried to swim out to where he was but it was too far. All of a sudden a lot of blue water came up, real blue it was, and we knew that an octopus had got him and taken him out to sea to eat. We had to go home and tell his family.*"

The fourth instance was in the orchard of Penty-Bryn, before it became a hotel, when a young lad from a local family hanged himself from one of the apple trees.

On a lighter note Will Jones recalled the innocent mischief that he and his friends used to get up to like playing knick-knack on people's windows. This seems to have involved a needle threaded with heavy cotton and coated with wax. It would be stuck in the putty and tap, or knick-knack, against the window. Will also recalled playing tricks on the local policeman... PC Benney.

THE OPERETTA "FLOWERLAND. MOUNT HAWKE. 1924-5.

The Operetta Flowerland performed by the children of Mount Hawke in 1924/25
(We have included the names as written but identification of people in the back two rows is
rather confusing)
Back row (L to R): Mabel Walters, Pearl Tippett, Enid Rodda, unknown, Doris Bennetts (with wand),
unknown, Doris Tonkin, Cora Jones, Vera Mannell & Evelyn Chynoweth.
Third row: Phyllis Parsons (with posy), Dorothy or Mary James, Phyllis Tippett, Iris Carlyon,
Doris Gilcrest, ? Jose, Kathleen (Kay) Carlyon, ? Parsons, ? Parsons.
Second row: Muriel Tippett, Marion Bennetts, Hilary Pearce & Betty Harper.
Front row: Olga May, Audrey Jones, Vida Bennetts & Elsie Parsons.

The sewerage system arrived a little later…in 1929 according to Mary
George. Frank Carpenter referred to 100 houses being connected to the
mains system in 1931 and an old chap, referring to the sewage farm in Park
Shady, said, *"I tellee what, they lot do say that when it come out tis fit to drink
but they that tell ee that, don't drink it."* Before this installation the village
relied on cesspits and maybe the odd septic tank.

The First World War became known as the Great War and spanned the years
1914 to 1918. Like most communities Mount Hawke was expected to do its
bit and on the 8th April 1915 a recruiting rally was held in the village, at the
Council School, with a reception by the Reverend J H Beecroft.

Mount Hawke suffered its losses and the inhabitants erected a Cornish
Cross in memory of the men who had made the supreme sacrifice.

The church logbook states, *"The cross has a carved head and is built on a
concrete foundation. It stands inside the gates leading to the cemetery on unap-*

propriated ground which was specially dedicated. Forty-four persons from the village and immediate vicinity served in the war and in addition to the cross a framed engrossed scroll containing the 44 names was placed in the church. A similar one was also placed in the Wesleyan Chapel.

The arrangements for the memorial scheme were made by a representative committee with Captain John Goyne (Chairman), Mr J W Langdon (Treasurer) and Mr E J Oats (Secretary)."

The memorial bears the inscription, "In revered memory of William Blackney, William James Ely, Eldred Leonard Mannell, Herbert Pryor and Ernest Richards who fell in the Great War, 1914-1918."

The Reverend Frank Edwards of Newquay performed the unveiling ceremony which was preceded by a service in the Wesleyan Chapel conducted by the Reverends Beecroft, Edwards and Hickson.

Ashley Rowe referred to the re-population of the village after the Great War. "The housing shortage was general in most parts of the country but in Mount Hawke there were empty cottages." He suggests that the fact that each had a water supply was the reason that they were quickly brought back into use.

There are many Celtic stone crosses in Cornwall but some have disappeared like the one John Kinsman refers to in The Cornish Handbook, "The Short Cross which gave its name to a portion of the village of Mount Hawke, stood, some sixty-five years ago (written in 1920), at the junction of the roads leading from that village to the sea at Porthtowan, to Redruth and to Two Barrows respectively."

Joan Chynoweth remembered electricity coming to the village…in 1927. This was quite early and said to be because the village was on the direct route of a supply for Wheal Kitty Mine. She said, "Mount Hawke was a very different place in those days, we were surrounded by farms; there were a lot less houses and I knew everyone. I remember too when Wheal Kitty closed, there were a lot of local men out of work."

Annie Pope was a village character, every week she walked to St Agnes to collect the Parish Pay (2/6 per week) for old people. Each recipient paid her one penny. (W I 1950)

During the 1930s the village was policed from Blackwater, it was PC Cox who kept a watchful eye on proceedings.

Property prices have increased by leaps and bounds but if you had £142 to spare in 1942 you could have purchased a six-room cottage in Banns Vale Hill.

Henry Peters lived just up the hill from Phil Jones' cobbler's shop, where Monty & Sharman Burrows now live. It was two cottages in those days and he lived in the one nearest the road. Claude Tonkin recalled Henry shouting to them as they walked by, *"Come in here boys; now go across the road and get me a ha'poth worth of nicies."* Claude said that his favourite nicies were winter mixture sweets and he always gave them a few for fetching them.

Claude recalled some of the fun that the boys had in the 1930s like fishing for trout at Gover with Mrs Bennetts, Mrs Gooding's mother. He said, *"We used to catch some that were four or five inches long and bring them home for tea. We also made our own stilts out of a couple of cocoa tins held up with string but my favourite was the iron hoop or if you didn't have one of those you used an old bicycle tyre. This was rolled along the ground with a shaped metal stick called a drill and the favourite joke at the time was, 'Are you going to walk or trickle your hoop.'*

We couldn't afford a bicycle so I made my own out of an old frame I found. I fixed a cycle wheel at the back and an old pram wheel at the front, neither one had a tyre on it. It had no brakes and made a hell of a din.

Bertie Thomas was a friend and used to come down to our place to work the Magic Lantern. It was our machine and slides but he would operate it. Park Shady was a lovely place to play; we used to go down there to collect chestnuts."

A pig-sticker completes his gruesome work at Beacon View in Rope Walk

The advancement in aviation and aerial combat brought the Second World War into everyone's living room and although Mount Hawke does not have the array of wartime stories that exist about other parts of the parish its residents were greatly involved. The war memorial records those lost in the conflict: Reginald John Barkle, Ralph Carpenter, Harold Carter, Joseph Norman Eslick, George Edgar Pascoe, Alfred John Roy Pearce and Henry Stephens. In addition, the name of Joseph Henry Knight appears on the roll of honour in the church.

Arthur Roberts, in his Wartime Diary, includes an item on the 6th December 1942, *"Early this morning a plane crashed at Porthtowan, it flew into the cliff west of the porth and blew up."* He also recalled the 6th June 1944, *"For a long time we have been looking for this day. Last night the Invasion of France started and so far things are going well. It is very quiet around here, several hundred US coloured soldiers over on Wheal Charlotte Downs from Towan Cross to the cliffs in pup tents."*

On the 20th May 1941 Arthur recorded, *"There are more bombs over Park Shady and the next valley from Mount Hawke to Navvy Pit."*

Writing in the 10th Journal of the St Agnes Museum Trust, Stella Edwards from Gover Hill said, *"Opposite the cottage, where I lived at Gover Hill, there was a searchlight party during the war. In the dark I could see the rays of light going from left to right to keep an eye open for 'Jerries'. One night an incendiary bomb dropped at Towan Cross. I woke up terrified as Mother had stuck me in the spence for safety and it was dark and the bomb made the windows and the door fall off. The ARP (Air Raid Precaution) man used to bang on the door if we had the tiniest chink of light showing. Special blackout curtains were used.*

My father would interrupt our games with 'Hark!' which meant 'stop and listen!' We would all hold our breaths until he gave us permission to go on again. 'Only one of ours,' he would say."

In his book *Memories of Nancekuke* Ernest Landry wrote that the buildings at West Towan Mine were roofed over and a regiment of soldiers placed there. *"Searchlight crews were stationed around but it was quite a while before we had any German air-raids. Then one night we had one. They couldn't have been sure of the exact position of the Aerodrome (Nancekuke) and one bomb fell on Porthtowan beach, exploding a land mine there. They must have thought they had something big but most of their bombs fell on open country between Porthtowan and Towan Cross."*

Mary George recalled a plane crash at Gover. *"It was a fighter plane, one of ours, and the pilot was trapped in the burning wreckage; they couldn't do anything to save him. My father never slept that night."*

Dennis Barbary also had memories of the war; of a plane crashing just above Wheal Ellen Mine, in a meadow still referred to as Spitfire Field, of a searchlight position between Menagissey and Short Cross and of the old adit near Manor Parsley Mill being used as an air raid shelter.

Gordon Snell was a part-time hairdresser… it was his evening job. Donald Thomas was sitting in his chair one evening, in his shed next to the *Trenithick Corn Mill*, when Gordon said, *"There's a plane, it's one of Jerry's."*

They went outside and watched it fly in the direction of the Army Camp on St Agnes Head.

Donald said, *"We could see these little specks dropping from it and then we heard the explosions as the bombs hit their target. There was no returning fire but shortly after we saw a Spitfire overhead, doing the Victory roll."*

Lorna Rundle (née Mewton) recalled a mock invasion during the middle years of the Second World War. She said, *"I think it was a rehearsal for the invasion of Europe, there were troops all over the place and a load of 'prisoners' at Henly House. It was all over in the one day and they certainly left a lot of mess behind."*

Neddie Mewton built a concrete air raid shelter in the garden at the rear of the butcher's shop but it seems that it was only used on one occasion, Young Lorna, Edwyna and an evacuee girl took cover there as a German plane came in across the village and flew over Park Shady and Towan Cross. Doris Nicholls had been evacuated from Plymouth which, of course, was heavily bombed. The extent of her panic was alarming to the other girls but understandable as a short time earlier she had emerged from a shelter near her home to discover the bodies of her mother and brother.

Lorna and Edwyna with evacuee Doris Nicholls (right) outside the bungalow and butcher's shop

Mount Hawke Wartime Committee
Back row (L to R): Mrs Edith Pheby, (Archie Pheby's mother), Olga Thomas, Mrs Jolly (Bill Jolly's wife), Mrs Reynolds, Audrey Gribben, Bill Jolly, Mrs Harvey (farmer from Rope Walk), Mr Reynolds, unknown, Francis Garland and unknown.
Front row: Hetty Kinsman, Delly Snell (Gordon Snell's wife), Mrs Jelbert (Henly House), Mrs Nellie Pearce, Ernest Rodda, Mr Farr, Mrs Garland, unknown and unknown.
(source Mary Rodda)

Len Field was born in the East End of London and in September 1939 the combined efforts of fate and Adolf Hitler brought him to Mount Hawke…on a holiday in the country as he was told. Len was eleven, his brother two years younger and his sister just five.

Pause for a moment if you will and imagine your children or grandchildren being placed in a similar situation. With the threat of invasion hanging over the country they could not have been sure if they would ever see their parents again.

Len was told that he was responsible for his siblings and, with a large brown label pinned to their coat lapels and carrying their gas masks, they set off on this new adventure.

Len picks up the story. *"We travelled from the East End to Paddington Station to board a Great Western Railway train. Nobody seemed to know where we were going except the train driver, of course. All I can remember is hundreds of children on the platform in long queues; some were in a state of panic and many were screaming,"*

Len described the journey down to Cornwall as a mix of adventure and trauma. They eventually arrived in Truro where they were fed, watered and washed before being consoled with helpings of jam and cream sponge. They were then divided into smaller groups and Len, clinging to his brother and sister, was transported to the church hall in Mount Hawke.

"We were now ready to be presented to the residents of Mount Hawke... I held onto my brother and sister as I noticed one or two families being split up and showing great distress; very few residents took more than one child. Waiting to be chosen was a nerve-racking ordeal.

Mr and Mrs Ernest Rodda and their daughter Mary of Westwood, Menagissey, chose me but that meant that I was separated from my brother and sister. This was concerning for me and distressing for them.

My brother was billeted with Mrs Reynolds of Arbor Cot and my sister with some nice people in the village but she screamed all night for me. The following day Mrs Rodda agreed to take her as well, she was very kind.

Living on a farm was a completely new life for me. The house was large compared to our flat in London and with electric light, a bathroom, and beautiful views from my bedroom window, it was like heaven. Warm milk direct from the cows, Mrs Rodda's cream and homemade bread and cakes will never be forgotten.

I was taught to milk the cows, mainly Shorthorn and Guernsey, all by hand of course. This became a daily job for me, helping Mr Berryman, a local farmer... I enjoyed helping Mr Rodda to take his two horses to the blacksmith where I was allowed to fan the forge with large bellows.

Mr Rodda had a well-trained Collie dog, Gyp, a hard worker and good friend. Ratting in uncle Dick's barn and fetching the cattle were his favourite and best talents. Playing with Gyp on the farm was far better than in the streets of London.

Mount Hawke School was not very pleasant, too much singing, not enough mathematics and far too much punishment. It was a very strict school, not the wishes of Mr Fielding and Mr Doran who had travelled down with us but of the headmaster and his wife who had arrived from London with a new phase of evacuees. To my amazement he appointed me head gardener and, bearing in mind that my knowledge of gardening was limited to sweeping the concrete in our London back yard, his choice was not only ambitious but also eventful. I cannot remember any of the children taking any produce home; the headmaster and his wife perhaps took advantage of it. The disadvantage of holding my position was that when I failed I was severely reprimanded despite having no control over the climatic conditions. I could never win in that garden.

I joined the church choir. The Vicar was the Revd Greaves and when everyone else stopped singing he would continue, he was very deaf but an extremely nice man. I enjoyed being a choirboy and when I wasn't singing I was pumping the organ for Gertrude Rodda, the organist. She had a wonderful voice but she could be grumpy especially when she was playing the organ at a wedding and I forgot to pump. It made a terrible noise causing giggles from the congregation. I was usually preoccupied peeping through the curtains at the bridesmaids.

What an extreme contrast to my life in the East End of London. It is sad to say that it was the war which changed my life for the better at a time when so many other poor people were suffering. I was totally oblivious to the misery throughout the world.

Mrs Rodda took me to Truro one day and it turned out to be a wonderful surprise, my mother had come to Cornwall for a holiday away from the London blitz. After her holiday she stayed on and eventually moved into a small cottage in the village. Soon after, she gave birth to her fourth child, a girl called Mary who tragically died of diphtheria when she was five years old … on Christmas Day 1945.

Mount Hawke has changed so much over the last fifty years. Perhaps because I was young and enjoying my time there, it is easier to recall the good things about the village; it is all so clear to me. The tea-treats in the field at the back of James' shop (now LONDIS), having my hair cut by Gordon Snell for 6d (2½p) down by the mill; he could always tell a tale. Taking my shoes to be repaired by Phil Jones in his corrugated black shed which still stands on the corner of Penhall Lane, later owned by Archie Pheby. Miss Rowe ran the village store and Mr Mewton the butcher's shop opposite LONDIS; he also worked on the threshing machine during the harvest. Sadly the blacksmith shop is no longer there, it was demolished some years ago but I can still see, in my mind's eye, the extremely good looking blacksmith, Mr Monty Rodda, who apart from being physically strong, had a wonderfully strong singing voice. He was probably the envy of the other young men of the village at that time. What wonderful memories.

My sincere thanks to the Rodda family for choosing me and for all the love and care shown to me and to my sister, Joan, during that most impressionable period of our lives as evacuees."

The large number of evacuees at Mount Hawke School

The School garden during the Second World War

The word evacuee slips easily off the tongue, perhaps too easily to convey the extent of the pain and suffering involved. We tend to think of children of the current generation as more advanced and worldly than those of past eras but consider for one moment this five year-old child waiting on a London platform, label pinned to coat, gas-mask around neck and suitcase in hand. The parting was emotional, tearful, and now the wait, with countless others, for a train to take her to an unknown destination … to live with strangers. Joan had been told that she would come home again, when it is safe … she must have hoped that was true.

Consider also the feelings of her parents, saying goodbye to her for what may be the last time. The pain for them must have been extreme.

For some children it was traumatic. It was seen as a rejection and some never forgave their parents for sending them away. The enforced separation took them from their mothers and fathers for up to six years and many felt deprived of their childhood.

For others, perhaps the majority, it was an adventure and their evacuation had a very positive effect on their lives. With the benefit of hindsight we hope that they all recognised their parents' decision as an act of bravery.

Bob Monkhouse was evacuated to Mount Hawke and lived with Stan and Evelyne Miners; Evelyne was originally married to Edgar Rodda, the blacksmith. Ann Rodda, her granddaughter, remembers playing football with Bob in the lane next to *The Elms* although, as she was quick to point out, *"He was ten years older than me."*

BOB MONKHOUSE OBE

18th June 1994.

Dear Phyllis,

Thank you for your letter with its kind
remarks about AN AUDIENCE WITH.....I am
so pleased you enjoyed it.

I will always treasure the memory of
staying at Mount Hawke with your mother
in law in 1944 and only wish the TALK
OF THE WEST was still there to provide
us with another rendezvous.

Best wishes,

Yours sincerely,

A letter from Bob Monkhouse to Phyllis Rodda

Local people covered essential roles like the village Fire Brigade which
required Sunday afternoon practice and marching drill at Truro. Mary
George recalled that Mr E Mewton was the Chief Officer and others in the

brigade were G Roberts, G Snell, W Carlyon, C Pearce, F Garland, J Varker, H Wilkins, G Mannell, H Thomas, M Parsons, J Durrant, W George and D George.

There were also two Special Constables…J Rowe and H Pearce and two ARP Wardens…P Kestle and M Tregunna.

In December 1946 the Women's Institute members wrote about the end of the war, the departure of the evacuees and the gradual adjustment to the peace. Despite the rationing and shortages there was hope for a better future.

Lorna Rundle (née Mewton) said that Saturday nights in the 1940s were a bit noisy with lads returning home from a visit to the Victory Inn. A regular prank was to swop gates and the next day Penty-Bryn's could be found at the church and vice versa. Folk had to search the village to find theirs. Will Jones also referred to this so it was going on before 1920. It seems to be something that lingered as it was still happening in the 1950s.

Donald Thomas recalled Bob Blitchford, an ex Royal Navy man who lived at Banns, almost opposite *Trenarth*. It seems that he grew tobacco, "Rows of it," said Donald. "It was about four feet high and he'd pick off the bottom leaves and hang them up in his greenhouse to dry. When they were ready he'd coat them with a mixture of treacle, saltpetre and rum, wrap them in hessian and tie them up with fine string. After a few months he'd remove the hessian and string and it was ready to be cut up and smoked in a pipe. I made some for my father but when I used rhubarb leaves I soon stopped, I found out that they were poisonous."

A blocked up window in an old cottage may well have been to avoid the payment of tax. In 1696, during the reign of William III, Window Tax was introduced. John Passmore Edwards of Blackwater considered it to be a tax on light and air and that it, *"Enfeebled the British race."* The tax applied to a house of more than six windows and to avoid it, window openings over the stated six were built up. Rodney Grant lives at *Shenfield* where there is evidence of this and despite the repeal of that particular tax law in 1851 the window remains blocked up.

The hunt gathers in the village before the off

Writing in the St Agnes Parish Silver Jubilee Programme E M Hymes reflected on the changes that had taken place since the 1935 Silver Jubilee of King George V when only three children under school age were living in the village. *"In 1938 the school closed having no more than 20 pupils. In 1939, with the outbreak of war, it re-opened and one of the evacuees attending was Bob Monkhouse…*

During the late 1920s and 1930s activities included tennis and football, a Cottage Garden Association holding a two-day annual show and a competition for the best maintained garden. The Men's Literary Institute then, and now, provided snooker and billiards…

After the war in which Mount Hawke was hit by a number of bombs, fortunately without loss of life, the village began to expand. The first Council Houses were built followed by two private estates and a chalet park… Community and Playing field Associations were formed and a Gun Club…"

Referring to the Council Houses in Short Cross Road, Edith Johns said that when they were built they stuck out like a sore thumb as they were so far out from the other housing. It is a measure of the extent of development that they are now well within the curtilage of the village.

Johnny *Winger* Barkle lost an arm in a farming accident when he was a young man but that didn't stop him working. He was a roadman; he cleaned the drains, trimmed the hedges and cleared the litter. He worked with a rope tied over his shoulder with which he supported his wheelbarrow.

Johnny Barkle on his motorcycle

For a number of years an anonymous benefactor issued a list of about twenty people who were to receive a free bag of coal at Christmas. A few weeks before the event George Tallack would enter the post office with the words, *"I've got the letter Pard."* One year the letter did not arrive and thoughts turned to who had died during the past twelve months.

Monty Rodda's name crops up on numerous occasions which is not really surprising as he was involved in many aspects of village life and was quite a character. He and Phyllis had three daughters, Ann, Carole and Diana all spaced well apart. As Ann said, it must have been the seven-year itch. Diana still lives and runs a business in the village.

Monty was driving down through the village with Howard Chynoweth as passenger when something whistled past them. Howard turned and said, *"Monty, a wheel just overtook us,"* to which he replied, *"Ess, Howard, 'tis ours."*

Ann recalled another occasion when her father arrived home and said to one of her boyfriends, *"Drive can 'ee? Here's my keys, the car's on the chapel steps."*

The telephone box once stood in the square, in front of what is now the LONDIS shop; no doubt because the post office had once been near there. Ann Rodda recalled that Nellie Pearce asked for it to be moved down the hill, outside where she ran the post office, where she could keep an eye on it. It seems that she had become aware that certain youngsters were making local calls free of charge, by lifting the receiver and tapping out the number. Pressed for names, Ann volunteered her own but claimed the Fifth Amendment on the others although Mike Pheby's name did crop up quite a lot.

A book of stories about the village was written by Mr Lamb, he lived in a cottage just below the entrance to Rope Walk. It has proved to be elusive but we are sure that a copy will surface after we go to print.

The youngsters of Mount Hawke were no different from those in other villages but there are a few names that seem to crop up whenever there is mention of a bit of mischief. Monty Burrows, Michael Pheby, Graham Parsons and Roger Hocking are some of those who have been raised in the village and enjoyed their young life there.

Monty, Michael and Roger often played in Gover Valley and one day they decided to block off the stream that runs from the bottom of Gover Hill, past the old corn mill, down through Banns and Park Shady. The exercise was a major success and the stream ran dry. Gordon Snell, who lived next to the corn mill, found his ducks stranded on dry land; he was not a happy man.

Mother's Day was a time for flowers and Monty and Mike decided on a bit of private enterprise. Armed with a hook and an old bath they set forth to cut down as many daffodils as they could find and it was not until Clifton Barkle caught up with them that they realised that there is no such thing as a free bunch of flowers.

Monty recalled one painful episode when they were down by the stream and it started to rain. John Hocking clambered into a chicken's house and closed the door. The boys were obviously disgruntled at being left outside so they pushed the shed across to the bank and tipped it into the river. Monty said, "The old shed must have been a bit rotten because it disintegrated and he was left sitting in the river with all the bits around him. He wasn't very pleased. We shot off but he eventually caught each one of us and had his revenge."

The death of Carole Rodda in April 1963 was a tragic blow to her family and a shock to the entire village; she was only seventeen. The Land Rover in which she was a passenger struck a wall and overturned. The funeral service was held at Mount Hawke Parish Church and six friends acted as bearers; Graham Parsons, Alan Green, Graham Carlyon, Monty Burrows, Peter Pascoe and David Warren.

In February 1965 Mount Hawke lost one of its best-known sons. Ashley Rowe was a Cornish historian of some standing; an authority on old Cornish rites and traditions who epitomised everything that the Old Cornwall Society stood for. He wrote many articles and a number of extracts are included in this book.

During one of the hot summers in the 1970s a large area of Park Shady caught fire and many villagers turned out to help the professional fire fighters. Alfie Johns recalled how frightening it was. *"We were doing our best to beat it down when all of a sudden the fire jumped across the ground and we were surrounded by flames. I never realised that it could move that fast. After it was over there were some grim statistics of the amount of dead wildlife in the valley."*

Each village in the Parish of St Agnes celebrated the 1977 Silver Jubilee of Queen Elizabeth II in its own way. For Mount Hawke and Porthtowan it was kite flying, a fancy dress parade, sports, dancing, gymnastics, a tea with the presentation of Jubilee Mugs and a football match.

In 1981 the country celebrated the wedding of Charles Windsor and Diana Spencer and for one eleven year-old it was success on a plate. Leisa Winstanley created a special design for a plate to commemorate the wedding. She had the pleasure of appearing on the BBC programme, Blue Peter, and to share a wedding present with the happy couple. Her design was made into a pair of plates…one for her and one for Charles and Diana.

County Council forester Paul Hurd led a team from the St Agnes Anti-Nuclear Action Group in a massive horticulture exercise in Banns Vale in 1982 when 1,000 saplings were planted to replace trees lost through felling.

Ellen Blackney celebrated a special birthday in January 1984; she was 100 years old. She had moved to the village when she was 18 and worked as a domestic servant and later as an assistant in the village stores. In a newspaper article she recalled the horse-drawn bakery cart from Perranporth and baking their own bread in the shop Cornish Range, 13 loaves a day except Sundays.

She recalled the great blizzard of 1891 when there was snow from one hedge top to the other.

She and her husband, William, had run a smallholding but he had been killed in France during the First World War. Her last six years were spent at Henly Residential Home; she lived to be 104.

John Jotcham said that she clearly didn't approve of the changing times as she declared, *"Tidn like when I was a girl, the maids now are forthier than the chaps."* It may have been the same old lady who observed of a couple who had been living together and were to be married. *"There's nothing new nor strange there."*

In 1985 John Hilton's design skills were put to the test when he was asked by Marcia Wilson from Banns to engrave a pint glass for her son's birthday. Her son was none other than actor Oliver Reed who had recently married Josephine Burge. John said, *"I got to know Basil and Marcia Wilson very well; they were aware that I engraved items for the customers at the Victory Inn. I designed a glass that had a filmstrip curling down and around in a spiral. Marcia thought that it would be a good idea if I could incorporate pictures of Oliver and Josephine so I engraved a wedding picture in each cell. It was the most demanding thing I have ever engraved. It was a huge relief when Marcia said that she was delighted with the result."*

Former suffragette Gertrude Stamp enjoyed her 103rd birthday at *Henly Residential Home* in June 1986. She celebrated with a cake made by Stella Williams and recalled her involvement in the campaign for women's votes.

In 2003 the village of Mount Hawke was catapulted into the world of show biz when one of its residents won *Fame Academy* and was awarded a recording contract with Polydor. Bookies' favourite Alex Parks was said to have, *"Stood out from the rest,"* and her win immediately catapulted her to stardom. Ironically she had not applied for the event, her father, Stephen, had submitted a tape and so began her long road to success.

While we were glancing at Diana Rodda's photograph albums we came across an item which we knew existed but had never seen, a piece of music entitled *Mount Hawke*. It is set to the words of the hymn *O for a thousand tongues to sing*. James Prowse holds the copyright and we assume that he wrote it.

In 2008 an item found at the western end of Park Shady, quite close to Navvy Pit, turned out to be a granite quern…a primitive object used to grind flour for bread-making. It was found on Mr Ealden's property, in field number 3917 and at a depth of one to two feet. It has now been donated to the St Agnes Museum Trust.

A small housing development is soon to be built in the field adjacent to the *Old School* public house. Beacon View was granted planning permission on appeal and most of the properties will be sold on a shared ownership basis to people with local connections.

So there we are, bang up to date. There comes a point when we have to shut up shop and say that any more submissions will have to be the subject of another book. We have reached that point.

Conclusion

Few Cornish villages have grown as rapidly as Mount Hawke and as we have gathered our information there have been many who questioned whether the speed of that change has been entirely beneficial.

In many ways it is similar to other areas of the parish which have lost their traditional industries of farming and mining. They have become commuter villages, where people live while working elsewhere. We have not carried out any research on the age structure but our feeling is that the fear that Mount Hawke would become a retirement village has not been borne out, there is a good spread of ages with plenty of youngsters for a long and active future.

Just like the other areas of the parish, we have enjoyed our dip into Mount Hawke life, we liked what we saw and wish it well for the future.

Circa 1904...Village children posing in front of Bessie Grigg's shop with the cobbler's on the left and the bus house opposite

Acknowledgements

We have been fortunate to enlist the help of many local people in this project, some in response to our request in *The Bolster*. They were all eager to see the history of their village in print. We have assiduously sought their recollections and appreciate the cooperation and help provided, particularly from those listed below. The chats and cups of tea have been enjoyable and from the reaction received, we have a sneaking suspicion that most people took pleasure in the chance to share their memories. Our thanks go to all those who have been so generous in giving their time to make this book possible. They have been sorely tested recalling the stories and identifying the people in the photographs … we sincerely hope that between us we have got it right.

Marlene Ball, Dennis & Margaret Barbary, Shirley Barrett, Monty & Sharman Burrows, Martin & Gill Caddy, Graham Carlyon, Margaret Carter, Chris & Hilary Chynoweth, Joan Chynoweth, David Collett, Jackie Cotton, David Docking, Len Field, Reverend Donald Forway, Donald George (unfortunately died before publication), Mary George, Rodney Grant, Josie Greenslade, David Hall (unfortunately died before publication), Edwyna Hall, Bob Hanson, Effie Harvie, John Hilton, Vivienne Honey, Nick Hopley, Carole Hunt, Mavis Hutton, Edith & Alfie Johns, John Jotcham, Carl Mills, Sue Morris, Eileen Murray, Wendy Norris, Penny O'Keeffe (née Tompkins), Oliver Padel, Christine Pearce, Mike Pheby, Peter Pollard, Ann Rodda, Diana Rodda, Mary Rodda, Lorna Rundle, Ted Skimins, Connie Stevens, Emma Thomas, Donald & Marcella Thomas, Gladys Thomas, Peter (Nick) Thomas, Tom Thompson, Claude Tonkin, Maureen & Robert Townsend, Lorna White, Peter Wilkins,

The scrapbooks and papers prepared by the members of Mount Hawke Women's Institute have been invaluable, a real social history. We are indebted to those who produced them and to the current members for permitting their use.

We must also make special mention of the work of Shirley Barrett in collecting information from a number of local people; many of whom had died before we started our work.

Our research has been greatly helped by the excellent staff of the Cornish Studies Library, the Courtney Library and the Cornwall County Records Office; these are invaluable sources of information for local historians.

Proof reading is an onerous task, you get it right and no one notices but get it wrong and it's there for everyone to see. A special thanks, yet again, to our good friend and mentor Alan Murton from Goonhavern for carrying out this onerous task.

The photographs appearing in this book are from many sources including Ken Young (photographer) and the extensive Clive Benney Collection.

References

Books:

A Millennium Chronicle...Frank Carpenter
Friendly Retreat...M H Bizley
From Death into Life...The Revd W Haslam
Memories of Nancekuke...Ernest Landry
Perranporth...Captain William Roberts
The Cornish Handbook...John Kinsman
The Metalliferous Mining Region of South-West England...H G Dines
Travelling to Truro...Roger Grimley

Other documents:

Mount Hawke Church logbook
Mount Hawke School logbook
The Journals of the St Agnes Museum Trust
The scrapbooks and writings of Mount Hawke Women's Institute
The jottings and notes of Shirley Barrett

Articles and extracts from:

The Journals of the St Agnes Museum Trust
The Royal Cornwall Gazette
The Sherborne Mercury
The West Briton

Books written by the same authors

Clive Benney:

St Agnes Parish 1850 to 1920 A photographic record
St Agnes Parish 1920 to 1950 A photographic record
Around St Agnes...The Archive Photographic Series
St Agnes...A Photographic History Volume 1 Down Quay
St Agnes...A Photographic History Volume 2 Village & Shops

Tony Mansell:

Mithian in the Parishes of St Agnes and Perranzabuloe
St Agnes and its Band
Camborne Town Band
St Agnes Golf Society

Clive Benney & Tony Mansell:

A History of Blackwater and its Neighbours
Jericho to Cligga
Our Village Church